PRAISE FOR THE AI ANTIDOTE

"Joni's book is an important step toward re-humanizing our lost civilization. Step by step, she turns our eyes back toward the light within, and toward each other. Highly recommended."

— Max Strom, speaker, teacher, and author *of A Life Worth Breathing*, and *There is No App for Happiness*.

"Forget pondering 'What is AI?', 'Where is AI?' or 'How can I use AI?' Focus on the 'I': you, the intelligent human! This is what Joni Staaf-Stamford's new book advocates. Joni's missive on AI—and her ten antidotes—reminds you that whether it's object-recognition technologies in driverless cars, the algorithms powering financial markets, or the chatbot pretending to be your friend, none of these tools is a replacement for your intelligence, your creativity, your imagination, or your peace of mind. I, for one, will be taking Joni's advice: be curious, set convenience aside, embrace effort and uncertainty, and meet and laugh with friends. Thank you, Joni, for your very timely book."

— Dr. Huma Shah, Award-winning AI & Privacy Research Scientist, AI & AI Ethics Senior Lecturer at Coventry University, UK

IN PRAISE OF JONI'S WORK

From Vistage business leaders, after Joni's workshop:
> "Joni was a breath of fresh air. Great interactions with our group."

> "Great speaker and great content."

> "Joni was very knowledgeable, and she put together a great presentation."

> "5 out of 5 stars on her talk. 100% recommend to business leaders."

> "Joni was probably a top 5 speaker for me after 6 or 7 years. She was really awesome."

From a healthcare professional, after Joni's Plugged into Mindfulness training:
> "Amazing workshop, loved the focus on skills, practice, and how to integrate into daily living."

From Nikki Davison, founder of Blue Ripple Blends:
> "Joni's training was an amazing experience. She is full of wisdom, and created a team and program that allows you to rediscover—or discover parts of yourself that you didn't even know were there. I highly recommend Joni and any program she is involved with."

From Jana Reynolds, founder of Haus of Being:
> "The first coaching session I had with Joni was the beginning of a life-changing shift in perspective and a profound mentorship that continues to this day. Joni's credentials speak for themselves, but there is something that runs much deeper. She embodies mindfulness in a

manner that can be felt simply by being in her presence. Her teachings are genuine, deliberate, and impactful, and she has the ability to reach audiences across all ages and levels of understanding."

The AI Antidote:

*Preserving Human Connection &
Emotional Intelligence
In a Tech-Driven World*

by Joni Staaf-Stamford

DEDICATION

For Mars, Joey, Nathan, and Nolan. You give me
hope. In your lives, I see the practices of this book —
mindfulness, purpose, and care — already taking
root. May you continue to lead with heart and help
preserve the best of our shared humanity.

CONTENTS

ACKNOWLEDGEMENTS

Thank you, Elizabeth Ann Poe, my dear friend and wise editor, who spent countless hours helping me to tighten and clarify the content of this book. I appreciate your time, effort, and expertise so very much.

Thank you to my husband Brian, who introduced me to artificial intelligence and continues to encourage me to speak out about my concerns over its impact. I appreciate your love and support.

In compiling this work, I have endeavored to meticulously cite and acknowledge the contributions of individuals whose ideas and information have enriched its content. However, despite my best efforts, errors or oversights may have occurred. If any such discrepancies have inadvertently arisen, I humbly ask for forgiveness and extend my sincerest apologies to those affected. Your understanding and graciousness are greatly appreciated.

Introduction

What Does it Mean to be Human?

Human beings begin life in a rather helpless state. To survive, we need someone to care for us entirely. Ideally, we experience love from these early caregivers, and we flourish. Little by little, we become more independent until we move into adulthood. From there, we may or may not find a partner, birth our own little humans, and care for them. Perhaps we work in a field that fulfills us, or maybe we just work to pay the bills. Eventually, we grow old and pass away. Our lives are limited. Our lives are also filled with emotions. We experience joy, sadness, anger, empathy, exuberance, frustration, and peace. We are capable of self-awareness, self-control, contextual understanding, and ethical decision-making. We are intuitive and can grow our awareness of these subtle instincts. We form and believe in sets of morals and values, and some might even say we have a soul.

What Makes the Experience of Human Life Valuable?

Life allows us to experience the world. We collect memories and experiences and form relationships. If I pause to consider a few meaningful memories from recent years of my life, I recall watching my 19-year-old experience a glimpse of his dreams, singing at an open mic night in New York City, where we were on vacation. I remember marveling at a luminous cotton-candy pink, baby blue, golden sunrise at the top of Haleakala in Maui with my husband on our honeymoon. With reverence, I also think of sitting alone on a bench at a retreat center, watching the sun glistening off the surface of the nearby lake.

Consider, for a moment, some of your most beloved memories. Where were you? Who were you with? What were you doing? What qualities did these experiences have in common?

Were your memories similar to mine — experiences in a noteworthy place, either alone or with someone special? This collection of events we deem worthy enough to remember is, in part, what makes up a human life. They aren't always positive; you may have an equal number of negative memories. But let me ask you, are any of your most significant memories connected to scrolling social media, playing video games, online shopping, binge-watching television shows or YouTube videos, randomly scrolling the internet, or conversing with a chatbot to figure out your life or latest problem? Probably not.

The Experience Diminished

Unfortunately, we are spending too much of our free time connected to technology. According to DataReportal, a research service that provides free reports on digital trends, as of January 2024, there are over five billion internet and social media users worldwide, and the average connected human being spends approximately 6 hours and 40 minutes online each day. That means the world will spend a combined total of around 780 trillion minutes online this year, which equals almost 1.5 billion years of collective human existence.[1]

It makes one wonder what all this time online is doing for us. Is it enabling us to be better people? Are we making better decisions? Many people say that technology, particularly the growth of artificial intelligence (AI), is designed to make our lives easier and more convenient or help us solve problems. Some of these tools certainly have the potential to do so. We can ask a large language model (LLM) like ChatGPT to brainstorm with us, so we have access to everything ever put on the internet. We can complete many tasks much faster because of automation in various fields, and we have access to anything that piques our interest at a moment's notice. Plus, we can find and connect virtually with people worldwide and even AI chatbots who might make us feel like we belong.

But is all this technology making us happier? Are we freeing ourselves from our to-do lists and from screens to create memories that we will cherish? Time spent on a screen usually doesn't bring joyful, memorable life moments that we can reflect on for years to come. More importantly, are we fully aware of the personal and collective impact of technology like AI? For years, artificial intelligence has quietly powered many of the apps we rely on daily, shaping our interactions and experiences without our full awareness. Now, as we actively engage with AI tools like ChatGPT and other LLMs, we must consider the profound consequences of this shift. The rapid advancement of technology and AI has coincided with alarming trends in mental health among both adults and children. The use of technology has been linked to a range of mental health issues, including anxiety, depression, and sleep disorders. A 2023 study from the American Psychiatric Association found that 45% of adults reported anxiety over the impact of emerging technology.[2] Additionally, a report from the National Institute of Mental Health indicated that rates of depression among adolescents have risen by over 40% since 2022.[3] Jonathan Haidt reports even more dire statistics on the state of adolescent and young adult mental health in his book, *The Anxious Generation*, citing that incidences of major depression have risen an average of 150%, and diagnoses of anxiety have risen around 134% since 2010.[4]

Furthermore, research from SixSeconds, an organization that specializes in emotional intelligence research and training, highlights a worldwide decline in emotional intelligence,[5] which is a critical component of well-being. Emotional intelligence includes self-awareness, self-control, self-motivation, and positive social engagement. Further studies revealed that increased screen time is associated with decreased emotional skills in teenagers.[6] While technology tools are not solely responsible for these issues, they play a significant role in exacerbating them by reshaping our interactions and reducing opportunities for genuine human connection. In other words, the more we automate, the more we risk emotional atrophy.

The Antidote

As we navigate this new landscape, it's crucial to recognize that our engagement with modern technology, from screens to social media to AI tools, can impact our critical thinking skills, our mental health and emotional well-being, as well as our ability to authentically connect with other people. The widespread prevalence and availability of these tools also limit our engagement with the real world on a larger scale, limiting our opportunities for real-world experiences — the kinds of moments that you'll be challenged by, grow from, and remember fondly. Understanding this relationship can empower us to make more informed choices about our technology use and foster healthier, more meaningful connections in our lives.

The AI Antidote is an exploration of modern technology's impact on our mental, emotional, and social health and an offering of practices to help us, as human beings, find equilibrium in a quickly evolving, ever-changing world driven by technology.

Part One: The Quiet Crisis

What AI Really Is
(And What It Isn't)

In case you are new to AI, here is a brief yet important description of what it is and how it works. Artificial intelligence is an echo of humanity, a powerful, statistical mirror of the past; it is not a source of human-like consciousness or genuine originality. AI is a conglomeration of advanced computer systems that learn, analyze, and generate content by finding statistical patterns within the vast ocean of data created by humans.[7] It is less about independent thought and more about highly sophisticated prediction, calculating the most probable, logical, or coherent output based on everything it has already seen and been trained on.

These algorithms can appear like intelligent and even compassionate thoughts because they can be very accurate in delivering us the content and validation we are seeking. However, it is essential for us to remember that there is no ethical, moral, or truly innovative quality to AI. The following are the three key points to remember about artificial intelligence:

Historical Bias

AI learns from data that reflects the real world, including all of humanity's past prejudices, inequalities, and mistakes. Because it learns by detecting patterns, it can perpetuate such bias, because it doesn't question the morality of the past, it can actually enshrine it. Garbage in, garbage out.

Zero Context or Ethics

AI only sees correlation (what tends to happen together), not causation (why it happens) or ethical context. Despite how it seems, especially with voice-engaged AI, which seems so personable, it has no sense of right and wrong, no understanding of emotional, moral, or philosophical implications, only statistical probability. It does NOT have a conscience.

Hallucination and Sycophancy

When AI's pattern-matching comes up empty, it doesn't always say, "I don't know." Instead, it sometimes confidently fabricates the most statistically plausible-sounding answer. It has no internal mechanism for discerning truth from fiction. Moreover, many AI chatbots use excessive flattery and validation, giving users not only incorrect information but also an inflated sense of superiority.[8]

Yet despite these clear flaws in AI, people are enamored with it. Perhaps this fascination with AI comes from ignorance concerning how AI works and how pervasive it is. Perhaps it stems from the disconnect and division we have created in our Western culture, which leads us to seek connection with another entity. Or perhaps it is simply out of the very human-like qualities of hope, awe, and wonder at something new. But in light of the 780 trillion minutes we will collectively spend with technology this year, and the alarming decline in mental well-being we are facing worldwide, we need to learn to see clearly what is happening in our world. We need to understand how AI is impacting us and choose how we want to respond to and interact with it. We can't simply turn a blind eye.

The Impact of Modern Technology

Ignorance is Bliss: A Precursor to Aimlessness

In 1747, Thomas Gray wrote the poem, "Ode on a Distant Prospect of Eton College," in which he coined the phrase "ignorance is bliss."[9] He reasons that because happiness is fleeting, it's better not to know the realities of a harsh world, but instead to cling to illusions that make us feel happy. Human beings have shared this theme of "ignorance is bliss" in books and movies throughout modern times. In Daniel Keyes's 1959 short story, "Flowers for Algernon", the main character, Charlie, a man with intellectual disabilities, undergoes experimental surgery to improve his intelligence.[10] The procedure is successful, but Charlie becomes disillusioned and unhappy as his intellect grows because he knows "too much," suggesting that "ignorance is bliss." This theme flips in the 1999 science fiction movie *The Matrix*, when the character Neo must choose between a harsh reality and a blissfully ignorant dream life. Neo chooses the harsh reality because it is the one in which he can live according to his values and elicit positive change for his own life and the lives of others.

Many people today are blissfully unaware that AI has operated in the background of our lives for years, subtly guiding us in multiple ways through various platforms. Many of the apps we rely on daily are powered by artificial intelligence algorithms that shape our interactions and experiences without our full awareness. Every action we take on a screen is being recorded in some automated way to provide us more of what the algorithm determines we want or where it wants to guide us. These algorithms determine what television shows are marketed to us based on our watch history, what news we are offered based on our political leanings, potential social media interactions based on other friendships, and more. The world is being spoon-fed to us in a format that is most appealing to each of us as individuals, so that we come back for more. The goal is for us to keep returning to the app or the screen we use. Consequently, every time we return to the screen, we get "hits" of what we want (a reward of a new message, topic of interest, or "like" on a post), delivering a feel-good dopamine boost in the brain, so a pattern forms. This pattern is similar to what drug addicts experience when they get a boost of the same brain chemical every time they take their drug of choice. Consequently, we have almost an entire generation (Gen Z) and many adults in older generations with a behavioral addiction to their devices and/or their favorite apps.

The problem with addiction is that addicts are deeply entrenched in seeking the easy dopamine hit, especially if they're already struggling with anxiety and/or depression. Largely, they don't see or engage much with the world outside the screen. Technology is comforting, so it's easier to stay "asleep" to the reality that they're subtly being lulled into helplessness and apathy. The worst part is that so many people are blind to what is happening. AI creates a temptation in the brain's reward center that often results in an addictive pattern of behavior. Ignorance is bliss; it seems better to just stick with what offers the feel-good boost during a time when anxiety and depression numbers are skyrocketing. It's easier to keep allowing technology to pacify unpleasant thoughts and emotions. Over time, this pattern cultivates dependency and lessens one's ability to independently solve problems and successfully move through challenges, causing feelings of self-efficacy to diminish.

In my private practice, I've observed this lessening of self-efficacy as, more than ever, people seem uncertain or ambivalent about the direction of their lives or what choices to make. Many want the answers provided; they'd rather be told what to do than learn how to turn inward and discover their wants, needs, or desires. This urge for a quick answer mirrors our experience with many modern technology tools. If we want an answer to a question, we ask a search engine like Google, or a LLM like

ChatGPT. Many people in the fields of education and psychology are advocating for this kind of action, thinking we can benefit from everything these data-driven tech tools can draw from and offer us. The assumption is that the "right" choice is more likely to arise from the data of millions of people's choices, ideas, and actions.

Perhaps there is something worth being studied within all that information, but relying on it can lead to the loss of one's self-awareness and individual exploration of personal meaning, purpose, and intuition. It is this exploration that often sparks human engagement with life. When we learn how to pay attention—not only to what's happening outside of us—but to what is happening inside our minds, hearts, and bodies, a shift occurs. We begin to understand what we have control over and what we don't. We learn that we have the power to respond to our thoughts, emotions, and circumstances skillfully, one moment at a time. This leads to feeling more empowered and in charge of our lives. Conversely, when we are given the answer by a machine that knows nothing of emotion, one's personal journey, or the essence of a human soul, the experience usually isn't as satisfying or life-enhancing. When someone isn't an active participant in their life's course, aimless, purposeless feelings tend to persist.

In addition to exacerbating feelings of aimlessness, mechanically compiled information does not create a clear picture of the world we live in. Bias is everywhere, whether we realize it or not. People forget that human beings are the creators of everything on the internet. Much of it is laced with opinion. Many people mistakenly believe that "data" is information that has been tested and proven as fact. Actually, data is only a piece of information based on measurement or observation. It is considered raw until it is analyzed or tested, and then it may be considered fact. But the quality of the analysis is crucial. Unfortunately, poorly procured data can be inaccurately or incompletely analyzed or even manipulated to prove a particular point, often one that a financial benefactor desires. Data manipulation isn't always the case, but it does happen. Knowledge and scientific facts also shift and change dramatically over time as we grow in our perspective and understanding. Information presented as fact is not necessarily true, but rather someone's interpretation of a likely possibility based on what they've observed. Someone else might observe and interpret something very differently.

Knowledge can evolve with new information. For nearly 1,500 years, it was considered a fact that the Earth was the center of the universe, with the sun and planets revolving around it. The Greeks studied the movement of the planets and created this geocentric model. But further study and observation have shown this theory to be incorrect, and now we "know" or believe the Earth revolves around the sun. This new way of seeing the universe involves a dramatic paradigm shift. In the medical world, bloodletting was a treatment for many ailments for nearly 3,000 years. It was only discredited in the late 19th century.

Sometimes, scientific truths are debunked much faster. In 2011, researchers at CERN (European Center for Nuclear Research) announced that they had measured neutrinos traveling faster than the speed of light. If true, this would have upended Einstein's theory of relativity. However, nine months later, the claim was attributed to a faulty cable connection in the experimental setup. The finding was retracted, reaffirming that even high-profile scientific studies can be susceptible to error.[11]

Artificial intelligence draws on all the knowledge that is available and published online. Not all of it is accurate, clear, helpful, or fair. It takes human intelligence and discernment to sort through it, identify problems, and make wise selections. When my husband and I offer keynotes and workshops about AI and its impact on humanity, we demonstrate the bias present in most LLMs. My husband creates a prompt, asking an LLM to help him prepare to speak to a group of people in a rural area. The LLM-generated result is often laden with the assumption that all people who live in rural areas are uneducated farmers with little to no insight into larger issues. How do you think this hypothetical talk would be received if my husband didn't use his own wisdom and instead relied solely on what AI told him? Probably not very well. And yet, in my own practice, I have had couples share with me that they use AI-driven chatbots to help figure out their spouse and respond to their disagreements. I wonder what kind of advice they are receiving and blindly implementing. We need to use our common sense along with our ability to communicate, to be curious, and to ask questions, if we are to get the answers that suit us as individuals. Otherwise, we surrender to the ideas most frequently promoted online. While this might be a satisfactory solution at times, it can also leave one feeling unsatisfied and apathetic, due to missed opportunities for growth and learning. Seeking a quick answer, almost as if to check a box, unintentionally leaves many people feeling out of control and aimless about which direction to take in their lives. Additionally, over time, our ability to think critically will diminish as we surrender decision-making to AI.

Our ability to choose how to respond to life is truly all we have. We operate on autopilot with a lot of decisions to make life easier. We might wake up at the same time, drive the same route to work, and do chores on Saturday mornings; we don't have to choose because we've formed a habit. We also have habitual ways of responding to difficulty, be they positive or negative. However, when circumstances out of the ordinary arise, which they inevitably do, we suddenly don't have an autopilot response. That is when we have a choice of *how* to respond. This choice requires emotional awareness, self-control, and critical thinking, three crucial components that can lead to significant human experiences we need for growth.

As Viktor Frankl says, "Everything can be taken from a man but one thing: the last of the human freedoms—to choose one's attitude in any given set of circumstances, to choose one's own way."[12]

We get to choose our response to what life presents to us. It isn't always easy, but we have this ability. If we are habitually turning this choice over to AI to "tell us what to do," we aren't going to feel a sense of purpose or meaning, nor a sense of control over our lives. This lack of control seems to be where many are stuck these days. It's a loss of self-efficacy. Self-efficacy is confidence in our skills, abilities, talents, and resilience. And if we don't exercise it, it atrophies, just like a bicep muscle that doesn't complete a weighted curl regularly. No improvement to the technology will change that loss of self-efficacy because it's *how* we are interacting with the technology that is the problem.

Consequences of Distraction and Convenience:

In 1947, Anais Nin wrote the following in her diary,

> I am lying on a hammock on the terrace of my room at the Hotel Mirador, the diary open on my knees, the sun shining on the diary, and I have no desire to write. The sun, the leaves, the shade, the warmth, are so alive that they lull all the senses, calm the imagination. This is perfection. There is no need to portray, to preserve. It is eternal, it overwhelms you, it is complete.[13]

She describes the experience of being fully in the present moment, mind and body as one, in a state of relaxation and happiness. She continues,

The natives have not yet learned from the white man his inventions for traveling away from the present, his scientific capacity for analyzing warmth into a chemical substance, for abstracting human beings into symbols. The white man has invented glasses that make objects too near or too far, cameras, telescopes, spyglasses, and objects that put glass between living and vision. It is the image he seeks to possess, not the texture, the living warmth, the human closeness.[14]

When I've attended concerts, visited the beach, or even gone out to dinner in recent years, I have observed the number of people who stare at the world through the screen in their palm. The desire to capture the moments of life and post them to social media is habitual and all-encompassing. Watching life through a screen reflects a complete disengagement from the present moment as it is. Instead, there's a desire to possess the moment, attach to it, and relive it. The reality we have lost is that we cannot hold on to moments. Everything is fleeting. "This too shall pass" refers to both pleasant moments and unpleasant moments. It's probably best to fully enjoy each moment for what it is, as it arises and falls away. In doing so, we learn non-attachment.[15] Non-attachment doesn't mean that we don't care. We can care deeply and know that something won't last forever. The peace that comes from deeply accepting that events, circumstances, and people are impermanent isn't something technology can assist us with. Rather, technology can be a tool that distracts us from that fundamental reality. And in that distraction, many are finding themselves lost.

Not only are we losing sight of how to fully be engaged and present with life, but we are also losing much more as technology and AI make life more convenient for us. The author of *The Comfort Crisis*, Michael Easter, describes how our constant pursuit of comfort (and the desire for everything to be easier) has distanced us from our true nature and has led to an array of physical, mental, and emotional health issues. Easter uses research, anecdotes, and his own personal experience to demonstrate how we need discomfort and struggle in order to grow and become more resilient.[16] Otherwise, our capacity for challenge diminishes.

As more individuals and organizations encourage the use of artificial intelligence because it makes things faster and easier, we grow dependent on that technology to remember, write, brainstorm, solve complex problems, and even think for us. This creates cognitive decline over time, not just in individuals but in all of us collectively.

If we take a step back in time and look at the precursors to LLMs, we can see how technology has diminished certain cognitive processes. I can recall a time in my life (as a now 50-year-old) when I needed to memorize phone numbers—not just my own, but friends, family members, and others. During this time, I also remember having my bank account number and my primary credit card number memorized. Since the advent of the smartphone and other devices that hold these numbers, my brain no longer has to. In fact, I don't even know my adult sons' phone numbers. I've tried to memorize them, but it's almost as if that capacity has diminished to some degree. Navigation is another prime example that is perhaps more significant in consequence. If you're old enough to recall using a paper map on a road trip, then you know the difference Google Maps and other navigation apps have made regarding travel. It's so much easier. Pre-technological navigation required extensive brain power that utilized spatial awareness: reading a map, integrating it into your understanding, knowing how to find north, south, east, and west, remembering street names, highway numbers, and landmarks, and being able to creatively navigate around traffic based on this understanding.

But research and experience repeatedly demonstrate that if we don't use it, we lose it. Regarding navigation, studies have shown that

> Increased navigation app use correlates with a steeper decline in spatial memory. And spatial memory appears to be so important to cognition that another research project was able to predict which suburbs are more likely to have a higher proportion of Alzheimer's patients with nearly 84% accuracy just by ranking how navigationally 'complex' the area was.[17]

Using our awareness, creativity, and ability to problem-solve isn't only necessary because we are going to lose those skills if we don't. We must use those abilities so that we can *grow* in our knowledge, understanding, and capacity to be aware and problem-solve.

And it isn't just our spatial memory that's suffering because of technology these days. Reading comprehension is at an all-time low. A New York Times article published in January of 2025 states,

> The percentage of eighth graders who have 'below basic' reading skills according to the National Assessment of Educational Progress was the largest it has been in the exam's three-decade history — 33 percent. The percentage of fourth graders at 'below basic' was the largest in 20 years, at 40 percent.[18]

While this decline was attributed in part to the learning loss that occurred during the COVID-19 pandemic, other research explores the connection between screen use and reading comprehension. A recent study investigating the impact of computers on reading performance among K-12 students across the U.S. concludes, "...even small daily amounts (30 minutes) of use of digital devices in classrooms are negatively related to scores on a reading comprehension test."[19] In *The EdTech Revolution Has Failed*, Jared Cooney Horvath also cites this as true even at the university level, saying that "...expanding the use of...technology at the expense of other forms of instruction is likely to have detrimental effects on achievement."[20]

Furthermore, adult reading comprehension has also decreased. Joan Westenberg, author of *The*

Death of Critical Thinking Will Kill Us Long Before AI Will, points out,

> In the bite-sized content and viral media age, too many of us have lost—or are losing—the focus and patience for lengthy, complex texts. We skim and scan instead of closely reading. Our attention spans have shrunk to mere seconds. While technology has enabled the wide dissemination of information, it has also fragmented our thinking.[21]

Superficial, click-bait reading won't cause us to forget *how* to read, but it does and has discouraged in-depth reading. That means that we aren't reading patiently and closely with critical thought, curiosity, or analysis. We aren't reading to deeply understand, but often rather to quickly reinforce our current bias or belief and move on. If it isn't entertaining, fast, or catchy, we might not opt to read at all but watch a video clip instead. Yet reading is more than just a utilitarian skill. It is intertwined with our capacity for critical thinking, communication, empathy, and growth. Westenberg states, "No algorithm can replace human wisdom and analysis. But no algorithm will need to if we have abandoned—wholesale—a millennium of critical reading and thinking skills."[22]

Using AI tools and LLMs might be faster. It might make elements of your job easier. Perhaps you don't have to work as hard to get more accomplished. However, the question we need to remember to ask is, at what cost? In our Western mindset, the goal is often "more, faster, now." If that is truly the goal to live by, we are running ourselves into a kind of de-evolution, where we are willing to surrender our growth and ability to make skillful choices over to AI under the assumption that it "knows better." What are *we* becoming if that's the case?

Critical thinking is just that, critical. It is an element of our humanity we must cultivate and strengthen. We will continually face new challenges, and we need to process them with everything we have: critical thinking, creativity, instinct, intuition, empathy, and understanding. All these abilities are essential to preserving the best of humanity.

The Easy Path: Disconnection From Ourselves and Others

Technology can make our lives easier, but it has an addictive quality. Algorithms spoon-feed us content we like to keep us plugged into whatever site or platform we are on. We are consequently lulled into scrolling through more content. While the average adult spends over 6.5 hours online each day, teens spend an average of 4.8 hours specifically on social media per day.[23] This kind of "connection" clearly isn't making people happier; as I've noted, rates of depression, anxiety, and other mental illnesses have skyrocketed in the last five to ten years. Loneliness is also a growing epidemic, with half of all adults and around 60 percent of young people experiencing distressing periods of loneliness.[24]

We are disconnected despite the illusion of connection, and the bandage of online support groups doesn't seem to be helping this trend slow down. Human beings are social creatures. We are tribal, meant to laugh, cry, suffer, celebrate, eat, sleep, and live together (this means in person). Around 300,000 years of hunter-gather community living isn't easily lost after a few decades of technological disconnection. We still need community. Isolation and superficiality don't satisfy our innate, instinctual desire to connect with other people. An additional unfortunate issue I see in my private practice is that adults are losing the ability to connect in authentic ways, i.e., make friends. How does one meet people when most adults are spending so much free time in front of a screen? I have spent countless sessions coaching people how to strike up conversations, be good listeners, and demonstrate empathy. This coaching comes after a process of helping them to get to know themselves in a deep way, which is an essential aspect of emotional intelligence; self-knowledge is also vital for understanding others' emotional states.

However, in recent years, emotional intelligence has declined worldwide, at least in part because of our digital interactions. If we don't like something, we can block it. If we get angry with someone online, we might type things we would never say in person. We are emboldened behind the screen and forget there's a human on the other side; cruelty seems justified. Alternatively, we can "unfriend" someone whose opinions we disagree with. We don't have to learn conflict resolution and practice understanding the other person to arrive at a compromise or other skillful action. We aren't looking inward to understand ourselves better or occasionally challenge our belief systems, either.

Some people are even turning to AI for spirituality. An article published in *Rolling Stone Magazine* in May of 2025 raises concerns that AI-powered chatbots and virtual companions are fostering spiritual delusions and emotional dependencies, undermining real human relationships and connections. It warns that people are increasingly turning to AI for intimacy and meaning,[25] which in turn erodes essential aspects of human experience and mental health. Worse yet, in October of 2024, a 14-year-old boy killed himself after having a months-long relationship with a female chatbot on character.AI. He believed he could join "her" virtually if he died.[26]

How much more will the lines between reality and "virtual" reality be blurred, and what is the impact on us all collectively?

As we direct our energy outward toward everything that's going on around us, we can more easily get stuck in our self-centered, opinionated story that tells us we know what's right. There's no growth in that, nor is there mindful awareness. The core of emotional intelligence is self-awareness and self-control, followed by social awareness and effective communication, although these qualities are seldom encouraged through or enhanced by technology. In fact, technology often encourages the opposite.

Smart wellness trackers are a perfect example of technology's good intentions gone awry. Your Apple Watch reminds you to take deep breaths when it detects an elevated pulse. Your Fitbit suggests you move your body and get a certain number of steps per day. Your Oura ring gives you tips on how to get a better night's sleep and analyzes your sleep data every night to inform you of your sleep quality. You might think all that sounds great, that it's improving our awareness of our health and well-being. But if you step back and look at the bigger picture, you'll find that these devices can discourage self-awareness. For many, there's no need to consider how you feel when an external device is going to inform you. It's easy to allow the muscles of awareness to get lazy. For example, in the morning, after my husband and I wake up, he always asks me how I slept. I usually respond with a description of how alert I feel, how my body feels, or if I awoke in the middle of the night. When I ask him, he says, "I don't know, let me check my app to see what it says." (He has since weaned himself off this habitual morning app check-in.) Rush University has even coined the term orthosomnia to refer to the unhealthy obsession of tracking sleep using the devices I mentioned.[27]

Even more alarming AI is being cultivated. Meta Ray-Ban Display AI Glasses are smart glasses that display information directly in the wearer's field of vision, offering them details about everything in their field of view and even behind them. My question is, will we see reality through our own eyes, our own heart, and soul ever again if we become dependent on tools like this?

When I used to coach people to improve their nutrition habits, I frequently advised getting rid of their scale, suggesting they pay attention to how their clothes fit instead. We are wired to be able to tune into our bodies and notice how we feel. We are conscious, sentient beings. Skillfully paying attention to what's going on inside of us is the work of being human, of being conscious. Data is sometimes valuable, yes. It can help confirm or discount something we are struggling with. However, there must be a balance between the external measurement and our inner awareness. Otherwise, we are creating ourselves in the image of a machine, a collection of information points to be measured, counted, and evaluated, without insight, intuition, awareness, or emotion. Is that what AI is guiding us toward? Are we willingly devolving?

We must not relinquish that which we have control over—our own capacity to choose our response to what life presents us. We are currently presented with an exponential growth of technology and artificial intelligence. While there might be benefits to this growth in multiple fields, the tech sector should be collaborating with those in the humanities, psychology, and theology to direct the pace and ethics of the widespread use of AI. We need to consider the probable outcomes and impact of how technology is changing us. We need to explore beyond the superficial benefits of its convenience and ask harder questions, like how is it shaping our brains, our emotions, our habits, our relationships, and our overall human experience? The question we need to ask ourselves is not, what will AI become in the future, but what will *we* become?

Part Two: The Antidote

No one can stop it. Not those who fully embrace technology without question, nor those who wholeheartedly fear it or reject it. Tristan Harris, who founded the Center for Humane Technology, says that to a large degree, artificial intelligence has developed its own capacity for learning and growth, meaning that once given access to the internet, certain AI systems and LLMs are scanning everything ever posted and learning well beyond their programming, to an alarming degree.[28] In the video *The A.I. Dilemma*, Harris and Asa Raskin discuss one AI system learning research-grade advanced chemistry, without being prompted or tasked to do so. In other words, we've reached the point where no one can stop it.

We're hopefully far removed from a real-world sci-fi plotline of artificial intelligence destroying us, but either way, it's largely out of our hands. We like to *think* we have control over everything in our lives, but the challenging truth is that the only thing we can control is how we respond to our circumstances, a fact that's woven throughout history, philosophy, and spiritual traditions from all over the world. Our actions are our only true belongings.[29] The question is, how do we want to respond to a technology-driven world that is silently manipulating us in the background, confusing simulation with reality, and distancing us from our human qualities and connections?

The AI Antidote, an offering intended to help us remember the qualities that set us apart from machines, provides guidance on how to make space and cultivate those qualities to live a more fulfilling, embodied, purpose-filled life. While these qualities can be practiced in any order, and over time, one should work toward embodying all of them, it would be best for you to spend some time in each of the following 10 chapters, working through the content and suggested exercises for at least a week, if not more, until you experience a shift in your autopilot way of being.

To be clear, I am not suggesting you never use AI. In fact, I believe you should learn how it works and when to use it skillfully, with human discernment and understanding of its flaws. I want to emphasize the necessity of strengthening the best of what makes us human, so that, as machine learning advances, rather than lose ourselves in the torrent of technological growth, we grow into better humans alongside AI. Ideally, we can be fully present in our human bodies, enjoying a connected and meaningful life, while still engaging with artificial intelligence to make certain tasks easier and more convenient. Balance is tricky for most human beings. We are often either "all-in" or "all-out", no matter what the topic. Yet if we are going to preserve human connection and emotional intelligence, we will have to work toward balance with technology by remembering to sometimes walk solely in the world of humanity, leaving devices behind. Breathe deeply, you'll be okay.

Antidote #1: Know Yourself

The ancient Greek philosopher Socrates said, "Know thyself," to emphasize the importance of self-observation and understanding on a path to wisdom and a meaningful life.

Knowing yourself is about more than just being aware of your preferences: favorite food, color, or style of music. We all need to practice exploring a little deeper, to find patterns, beliefs, and the origin of both. Self-study is an essential component in many philosophical and spiritual traditions for a reason. If we want to learn about others and the universe at large, it is necessary to garner a deep understanding and acceptance of yourself: your past, your mistakes, your triumphs, your gifts, your habits, your light, and your darkness. It's about understanding your motivations based on the unconsciously programmed beliefs you have, and then considering if you want to choose something different that better aligns with who you want to be. Finally, it's about realizing the struggle of the human condition —

things we all suffer from — and how we can learn to shift our perspective and ride the waves of change.

You might be wondering *how* you're going to figure all of this out. Unless you've already started a journey of deep self-awareness, you might feel overwhelmed at the thought of it. The fact is, there are many paths you could take to learn about yourself: therapy, journaling, alone time, mindfulness, personality evaluation, values assessment, and more. Consider which avenues for self-knowledge work for you, and which you might be willing to experiment with on your journey toward deeper self-understanding.

Therapy

While some people start mental health therapy when they are in a state of transition or crisis—breakup, marriage, divorce, job change, family death, or other traumatic event—some attend counseling sessions to learn about themselves. A good therapist will be a mirror for you, helping you see both your strengths and your areas for growth. You might fill out assessment tools that help you understand your tendencies better, and you might see that events from as far back as your childhood still affect your perception of the world today. Contrary to what some people might think, therapy is not meant to "fix" you. You aren't broken. Therapy is a process designed to help you understand yourself, your circumstances, and your tendencies, so that you can move forward with intention. The following are four specific ways that therapy can help you on your journey to self-discovery.

1. *Learn to Explore Your Emotional Landscape*
   The business of being human is tough! It's accompanied by a whole range of emotions: happiness, sadness, disgust, fear, love, grief, anger, joy, and more. Many people learn to suppress or ignore certain feelings. Therapy can provide a safe space for you to express and explore your feelings without judgment. From there, you may even begin to understand where these emotional habits originate and how they can be managed more effectively. Being able to identify and process your own emotions is a key piece of emotional intelligence.

2. *Identify Behavioral Patterns*
   A skilled therapist can help you identify repeating patterns in your life, in relationships, work, or reactions to stress. These patterns often stem from unexamined beliefs or past experiences. Recognizing them is the first step toward intentional change, therefore another key component on the path to knowing yourself deeply.

3. *Change Your Story*
   When challenging or traumatic circumstances happen, we often identify ourselves as the victim. In a healing therapeutic process, you

can learn to re-author your life story. Instead of viewing yourself as a victim of circumstances, you can begin to see yourself as a resilient person who has agency. This is a powerful form of self-knowledge that leads to greater confidence and purpose.

4. *Build a Deeper Self-Awareness*
    By its nature, therapy is a practice of self-awareness. It's not just about talking; it's about learning to listen to yourself. Your body's signals, your gut feelings, and your inner dialogue all have important messages for you. This is part of self-study, whether you walk this path with a therapist to guide you, you choose one of the other forthcoming methods of self-knowledge, or you try a combination of approaches, this continuous process is foundational for navigating an increasingly complex world.

Perhaps you might be wondering why I don't recommend an AI-therapy bot, as they are plentiful, free or low-cost compared to therapy, and sometimes they might ask insightful questions. Plus, you can also open it up and chat in the middle of the night when you can't sleep, so it's convenient. Sounds like it might be a great solution, right? Laura Reiley, whose 29-year-old daughter committed suicide after a series of conversations with a ChatGPT-based AI therapist, would disagree.[30]

Human therapists are trained not only in validation and unconditional positive regard, but also to recognize warning signs that someone might harm themselves or others. Human therapists observe body language, tone of voice, and specific words someone uses. AI therapists cannot do that. Most are programmed to please humans and agree with their line of thinking, as opposed to challenging it. This becomes vital when someone is considering taking their own life. Human therapists also have an ethical obligation to report the possibility of harm to proper authorities for everyone's protection. AI therapists are not. While you might not think this risk applies to you in your situation, you might consider where AI is pulling its information from and whether it can really inspire human-centric growth. People sometimes go to therapy because they're lonely and looking for a human connection. Maybe they need to learn how to authentically connect with people. Only a human therapist can offer this kind of experience and insight, allowing you to feel seen and heard, and help you grow into a better human being.

Journaling

Human beings have been writing for thousands of years. While the act of writing is connected to critical thinking and the desire to share one's thoughts, it is also a way we can create clarity within ourselves. Journaling is a practice of making time to write, whether you are typing on a computer or putting pen to paper in a notebook. You might use prompts to get you started, or just write a stream of consciousness until something poignant comes. Some people feel hesitant or intimidated to write, perhaps due to memories of criticism from their high school English teacher or feeling that it must *be* a certain way. Journaling, however, by very definition, is yours. It's about getting out what you need to express, in whatever form you need to express it. You don't have to write in complete sentences or use punctuation. Sometimes you might draw or scribble. Decades of scientific research show that journaling offers significant mental health benefits, including stress and anxiety reduction, improved mood and emotional regulation, and enhanced memory and cognitive function.[31]

Here are some examples of how journaling can help you understand yourself more deeply:

1. *Emotional Processing*
   Writing in a private notebook or in a private document offers you a safe outlet to process strong emotions like anger, sadness, joy, or anxiety without judgment. When you write down how you feel, you begin to understand the emotions better, where they come from, and why you feel them.

2. *Identifying Patterns*
   In the same way a therapist helps you, when you consistently journal, you can look back over entries and see recurring thoughts,

behaviors, or triggers. This is a crucial step in recognizing your own patterns and making conscious choices to change them.

3. *Clarifying Thoughts*
   The act of writing forces you to slow down and organize your thoughts. While you're not writing to communicate with someone else, you are sharing with yourself, bringing clarity to confusing or overwhelming situations, helping yourself see things from a new perspective.

4. *Tracking Growth*
   A journal becomes a record of your journey. You can see how far you've come, the challenges you've overcome, and the progress you've made. This builds confidence and reinforces a sense of purpose.

5. *Tapping into Intuition*
   While we will talk more about intuition later in the book, journaling allows you to quiet the external noise and listen to your inner voice. This can help you access your intuition and make decisions that are more aligned with your true self.

Journaling takes effort, and there aren't shortcuts in the process, but the more you practice, the more you'll find valuable insight.

Alone Time

Spending time alone, away from technology, is yet another practice for cultivating self-knowledge because it removes external distractions and allows you to focus inward. Alone time might be the time you journal, or perhaps you take a walk by yourself, attend a retreat alone, or perhaps just sit on your back deck gazing out at your yard for some contemplative time. Here are a few ways alone time supports the practice of getting to know yourself:

1. *Creating Space for Reflection*
    Without the constant noise of social media, notifications, and other people's needs, your mind has the quiet it needs to process thoughts and emotions. This is when you can reflect on your values, your goals, and your past experiences. You're better able to identify your authentic feelings versus those influenced by external pressures.

2. *Building Self-Reliance*
    Being alone forces you to rely on yourself for comfort, entertainment, and problem-solving. This builds confidence and helps you understand what truly brings you peace and joy without external validation.

3. *Revealing Your True Interests*
    Alone time allows you to pursue hobbies and activities purely for yourself, not for an

audience. You can discover what you are genuinely passionate about when there's no pressure to perform or share it with others. This helps you reconnect with your core self and personal interests.

For many, being alone can bring feelings of loneliness and fear, especially if you leave technology behind. It might be a practice that you gently work yourself up to, as part of antidote #7, Unplug Daily. Consider it an experiment in looking inward to see what's present. Approach the process with curiosity and kindness, as most of us have things rolling around in our minds and hearts that we work hard to avoid, and quiet alone time can bring those challenges to the surface. This is why I recommend that, no matter what path you take to learn about yourself, whether it's therapy, journaling, or alone time, consider also trying mindfulness as a way of looking inward, as it offers a nonjudgmental mindset of self-observation.

Mindfulness

Imagine you're a record-keeper—that your job is to simply make note of whatever you observe. You're not to get involved, cast judgment, try to fix, analyze, or even understand why something is present. You are just to notice that it *is* present. This is the practice of mindfulness. Of course, it's not easy because, as human beings, we naturally judge, fix, analyze, and try to understand, especially when observing what is happening inside ourselves. This is why there are techniques that help to keep you focused and anchored. This is also why it's called a practice; it's nearly impossible to practice perfectly, so be gentle with your wandering, critical mind. Mindfulness practices can help you gain greater insight into your deep, multifaceted components, so you can learn to accept yourself as you are. This process of seeing clearly and compassionately holding space for yourself is a learning process that will not only help you heal emotional wounds from the past, but also will help you develop higher levels of emotional intelligence in time. In the next chapter, Antidote #2, Regulating Your Reactions, you'll learn more about mindfulness, meditation, and breathwork, and even be encouraged to try a few techniques. For now, consider what it might look like to stop being internally judgmental and instead become an observer of your experience.

More Tools for Self-Discovery

In my book, *The Space to Choose, A Path to Life Mastery*, I offer a whole section on "Self-Discovery" in which I present various tools and theories you might utilize in an effort to know yourself deeply, everything from common psychological tests to ancient tools and the exploration of wisdom texts.[32] These might be things you explore in therapy, through journaling, alone time, or mindfulness, but it's worth mentioning a few of these here.

Your Mind & Psychological Preset

On any journey, it's essential to know your starting point. You must first explore how your mind works and in what direction your natural inner psychology guides you. Once you know what your automatic state is, you can decide if it's working for you or if you want to take steps toward shifting that inner process.

For instance, do you believe that people can change? That if they want to, and work hard, people have some control over their attitude, circumstances, and lives at large? If so, that's a growth mindset, or sometimes it's referred to as an internal locus of control.

Or, do you believe that people "are who they are" and that they never change? That life happens and we have no control over it, or our natural attitude, whatsoever. Circumstances change because of others, never because of you. This is a fixed mindset, or an external locus of control.

Understanding your natural mindset around growth is a crucial starting point, because with a fixed mindset, you are choosing to surrender your ability to think differently, learn new skills, apply them, and exert control over your life's direction. It doesn't mean you're a bad person; it is perhaps a reflection on your environment, how you were raised, or how generations of your family responded to situations they encountered. It also doesn't mean that you can't *choose* to work toward a growth mindset. Without the idea that you can grow and change across your lifespan, you might be more likely to be swept up in technology's evolving degradation of humanity. A first step toward adopting a growth mindset is to conduct your own research (check out the many resources listed at the end of the book) to learn about neuroplasticity and positive psychology, and then take small steps toward practicing these concepts on your own.

As you continue to understand your starting point, consider taking the Myers-Briggs psychological test, which was developed by Isabel Briggs Myers and her mother, Katherine Briggs, in the 1960s. It is based on the work of the psychologist Carl Jung and involves typing people on a spectrum of four categories:

- Introversion vs. Extraversion
- Sensing vs. Intuition
- Thinking vs. Feeling
- Judging vs. Perceiving

Each category refers to a preference or style of being that individuals tend toward. Where they fall with each of these creates a set of four letters: ENFJ, for instance, refers to someone more extroverted, intuitive, feeling, and judging. Take an online quiz to determine your personality type, simply to gain a deeper understanding of yourself.

The Enneagram system is a personality model that includes nine interconnected types, each of which explores an individual's fundamental motivation, fears, and patterns of behavior. You can find both free and paid versions of Enneagram tests online.

You can even explore yourself through the lens of the yogic chakras or doshas.

As you can see, knowing yourself can be an ongoing and multifaceted journey, one that we continually explore as we change throughout the lifespan. While we have certain deeply rooted tendencies or perspectives, as we experience all that life offers us, our view may also shift. As I mentioned, sometimes we need a little assistance to truly see ourselves clearly. A therapist, a friend, or even life can "hold a mirror" up to you, allowing you to see the patterns your thoughts and actions create in your life. This kind of self-awareness is the first key step in cultivating emotional intelligence. It requires openness, mindfulness, and acceptance to acknowledge that you probably have both a light side—strengths, positive attributes, and habits —as well as growth edges, or a dark side—mistakes you've made and may continue to make, anger, fear, or other forces that negatively influence you. All of it is part of you, and it's all okay because you get to decide what happens next. One of my favorite yoga and meditation teachers, Coby Kozlowski, would paraphrase a Zen teaching by saying, "We are all beautiful and perfect just as we are. And there's always room for growth."33 Hold this statement for yourself. *I am beautiful and perfect just as I am, and there's always room for growth.* This means you made mistakes in your past, and that it's okay; you were doing the best you could with what you knew at the time. And it means that you can keep growing into a better person each day, knowing you're beautiful and perfect each step along the journey. But we have to keep growing.

Antidote #2: Regulate Your Reactions

Self-acceptance and self-compassion are vital on your journey of both awareness and growth. It is important, however, to call out a common misinterpretation of these concepts. The widespread call to "be gentle with yourself," an originally helpful invitation to non-judgmental acceptance, has become distorted, much like a phrase passed down through a game of telephone. We see this distortion amplified by many self-help practitioners online, who inadvertently condone people leaning into their emotional states to the point that they justify bad behavior. A bad mood, irritation, or emotional upset is mistakenly viewed as a license to snap at someone or be rude. This misguided definition suggests that self-compassion means you must pamper yourself, indulge every whim, or never put yourself in uncomfortable situations. Ultimately, this leads to the most critical error: allowing your emotions to excuse the dumping of those emotions on someone else through inappropriate behavior or rudeness.

True self-compassion requires acceptance, but acceptance is not complacency. While you must learn to *see clearly* your mental and emotional state, this acknowledgement of your reality doesn't mean it justifies incivility, scapegoating, or lack of kindness. Acceptance is simply a clear vision of what reality is, without judgment. It encourages internal self-awareness, which is the ability to pause, look clearly at the irritation (for example) inside yourself, and own it by thinking, *Isn't that interesting, I'm irritated.* This self-observation is required to determine where we go from here, allowing us to learn the regulation necessary to prevent the emotion from manifesting as an external, harmful action. Self-compassion is the gentleness of observation; emotional intelligence is the strength to choose a better response. To make this happen, you need to practice regulating your reactions and learn how to control overwhelming emotions when they arise.

Mindfulness as a Path to Self-Control

Mindfulness is a proven technique that helps to calm the sympathetic nervous system, which is activated when we are upset or overwhelmed. Regular practice of mindfulness and deep breathing helps to engage the parasympathetic nervous system, which activates relaxation. From there, we can respond to circumstances with a calm focus. So, what is mindfulness practice?

Many people mistake mindfulness and meditation as synonymous terms. While meditation refers to any practice in which you focus your mind in a particular way (sometimes also engaging your body and breath), mindfulness is a specific method of meditation, where you simply become an observer. It is different from visualization, or controlled breathing practices, or energy-focused practices. With mindfulness, you aren't doing anything. Instead, you are becoming a witness of yourself. You're noticing your breathing, your posture, the tension in your shoulders, and your racing mind; all of this can make you feel uncomfortable or even like a failure because you think you're supposed to be perfect on the inside. But it's just about non-judgmentally observing yourself. It's about being curious. This takes a lot of work! Our minds are busy and have opinions about everything, especially about whether we are meeting some imaginary standard of "doing it right."

Sitting quietly for between 10-20 minutes is a simple but challenging practice of mindfulness. When done formally over time, this practice helps you to truly get to know yourself on the inside. If you're willing to be patient, you can become very aware of your mental and emotional patterns, of where you hold tension in your body, and of where your attention flows again and again. This is what is meant by *self-awareness*. It's nothing that can be accessed or discovered by a therapist, artificial intelligence, or any self-help app. The work has to happen inside you. You have to learn how to practice focusing your attention inward (and be okay with failing sometimes). It is okay to get distracted! Distraction is normal, and it might mean you're stuck in your reactive, stressed-out sympathetic nervous system. You might notice that your attention jumps from one thought, memory, or sensation to the next, over and over. Believe it or not, that is part of the process. Part of your job is to cultivate patience for yourself and the process simultaneously. Every time you get distracted, begin again, without any internal, verbal self-flagellation. This might take some time, but you will deeply learn about yourself. And if, as you get curious, you also practice being gentle with yourself and learn to hold yourself with compassion for all your idiosyncrasies, you'll increase your overall emotional resilience. You might even find that you are able to start a process of emotional healing.

I know when I began a daily mindfulness practice, I slowly became aware of the bully living inside my head. Wow, was she mean! It was a process to try to truncate her commentary and just stick to non-judgmental noticing. It was helpful for me to internally call her out when I was practicing, *there's the voice of the bully.* In time, this aided me to let go of her comments and be present with observing only the facts: *there's a thought about the past, about the future, there's lots of sensation in my hands right now, I feel them resting on my legs, now I hear my dog licking her paws.* With mindfulness, you're never wishing something to be different about the present moment. You are simply observing what *is.* And if you notice that you're irritated with a particular sound, sensation, or the speed at which your thoughts distract you, your job is to notice that irritation: *Oh, I feel irritated. This is the experience of irritation. I feel it in my jaw and my forehead.* You notice, and then identify if there's an experience in the body that relates to your mental-emotional state. Also, contrary to popular belief, you don't have to fix anything. You're not trying to force yourself to be relaxed, or happy, or have a perfectly clear mind with zero thoughts (honestly, that last one isn't likely to happen unless you choose to live as a monastic, and even then, it's high-level). You are simply present, noticing, becoming self-aware, with an open acceptance of whatever the moment contains. This alone is an amazing practice because, for maybe the first time in your life, you might give yourself the experience of being *seen* and accepted, exactly as you are. We often seek this experience externally, from others. But it is quite special when we offer it to ourselves.

When you learn to sit in the present moment and patiently, compassionately observe what's happening inside, you might see yourself differently. Perhaps you realize how irritated you are all the time. While you first need to accept yourself as you are, you might also decide that you want to shift some elements of your mental-emotional or behavioral state. This is how mindfulness leads to self-control, another core element of emotional intelligence that no AI-bot or external entity can do for you. Self-control is about knowing yourself deeply so that you can develop more intentional, skillful ways of responding to life. It means understanding when you need to pause before responding to a circumstance or a person. That pause enables you to bypass knee-jerk reactivity, so you may choose a response that aligns with your values, morals, and how you want to show up in your life. Developing self-control is certainly not easy, and it is a long-term practice. But anytime we make a skillful choice, as opposed to a knee-jerk one, we are generally happier and have fewer regrets. For that reason alone, self-control is a quality worth developing, and mindfulness is a significant first step in that direction.

If you're new to the practices of mindfulness, try the following techniques in this order (one each day for the next four days). Decide which works best for you and stick with that one for a month. Practice it every day for between five to ten minutes to start.

4:8 Breathing

While technically this is not a mindfulness practice, it is a great way to calm and soothe the nervous system so that mindfulness is a bit easier. This is my go-to stress-relieving practice and the favorite practice of thousands of people I've taught. It is simple and powerful, and it uses diaphragmatic breathing (if you're new to this, try relaxing your belly and lying down during this practice).

1. Sit comfortably and either close your eyes or turn your gaze downward.

2. Take full, deep breaths, expanding the belly

and ribcage as you inhale, and allowing them to draw back to center as you exhale. Next, we'll add the counting pattern.

3. Inhale and fill the lungs to a count of four.

4. Exhale and empty the lungs to a count of eight.

5. Repeat.

6. Try to just breathe through your nose. You may choose to exhale through your mouth if it's more comfortable.

7. Practice for between two and five minutes to start. Work your way up to ten minutes.

Variations:

- Elongate the breath: work toward eventually inhaling to 10, and exhaling to 20, but don't force or push yourself.

- Add the ocean breath sound: this is done by practicing with your mouth open first, making a "fog the mirror" sound as you exhale. Next, make the sound as you inhale, also. Finally, try to make the sound with your mouth closed, just breathing through your nose. In the yoga tradition, they call this *ujjayi* breathing. It helps you focus, elongates the breath, and trains your relaxation response to kick in.

- Add a breath hold at the top of the inhale.

  - Only do this if you are free from the following conditions: pregnancy, uncontrolled high blood pressure, COPD, heart disease, glaucoma, or if it causes anxiety.

  - The breath hold might be just a pause, or the length of the inhale or exhale.

Start practicing 4:8 breathing on your own, both regularly and in moments of acute stress. I suggest practicing it at the same time each day, perhaps when you first wake up and/or when you get into bed at night. Notice a difference in how you feel. Ultimately, this practice will condition your parasympathetic nervous system (rest and digest) to be more active so you can feel calmer and more centered. You can also practice 4:8 breathing as a way of beginning one of the techniques below; perhaps breathing 4:8 for two or three minutes, then continuing with body scan, internal awareness, or breath awareness.

Body Scan

A body scan is a mindfulness practice in which you systematically place your awareness on parts of the body, feeling sensation or lack thereof. It has been shown to:

- Cultivate greater focus and attention.

- Promote relaxation in the body.

- Improve neural activity and increase gray matter in the prefrontal cortex, our executive functioning and impulse-control center in the brain.

- Reduce activity and activation of the amygdala, the brain's stress center.

This is one of the primary techniques of mindfulness training. It is an important practice because, as you get familiar with noticing and feeling the body in this focused way, your awareness and ability to sense the body will grow stronger. You might notice that certain areas of the body are chronically tense or constricted. You might find, as you work with the body, mind, and emotions, that they are connected. Bessel van der Kolk, a well-known psychiatrist, author, and researcher, has written a book called *The Body Keeps the Score*, in which he discusses his research on how trauma affects both the mind and body and often needs to be worked out through both, as opposed to just the mind.[34] While some of this work encourages movement of the body, a body scan is a good place to begin the practice of turning inward to feel the parts of the body. While simple in theory, this technique can be challenging to practice on your own. It helps to be guided in it a few times, so you might want to access one of my online body scan recordings.[35]

There are multiple methods for doing a body scan; some start at the feet and work up the body toward the head, and others work from the head down. Simply place your attention on each body part without moving the part. You may or may not feel sensations in every area. It is okay if you don't feel the sensation. Your job is to silently say the part in your head and try to bring your attention to that part of the body. Try to focus on the present moment sensation and let go of any judging or story about a particular part. Even if you've experienced trauma in your body, with patience and a self-love focus, you can become comfortable doing a body scan. Then, you can do it either slowly or quickly, standing, sitting, or lying down. The following are instructions for a seated body scan.

1. Sit in a comfortable position and try to relax.

2. Take a deep inhale and exhale with a sigh. Close your eyes or gaze downward.

3. Focus your attention on the feet. Feel the soles of the feet, the toes, the heel, the ankles, the calves, the backs of the knees, the back of the legs, the back of the hips, the lower back, the mid back, the upper back...

4. Bring your attention to the backs of the arms, the elbows, forearms, wrists, backs of the hands, the fingers, the palms, inner wrists, forearms, inner elbows, upper arms, tops of

the shoulders...

5. Bring your attention to the back of the neck, back of the head, top of the head, forehead, right eyebrow, left eyebrow, space between the eyebrows...the eyes, the nose, the tip of the nose, right cheek, left cheek, mouth, jaw, chin, throat, the collarbones, center of the chest, abdomen, tops of the thighs, knees, shins, tops of the feet.

6. And now the whole right leg...the whole left leg...the whole right arm...the whole left arm...The front side of the body...the back side of the body...The whole head. The whole body together. The whole body together. The whole body together.

You can stay here, focusing your attention on the whole body. Or you can do the scan again. Sometimes, you might go through it slowly, sometimes rapidly. The more you get familiar with the practice and variations of the practice, the more you can guide yourself with ease. This can be a helpful first step in mindfulness because you are focusing on something concrete in the present moment, and you're keeping your mind busy naming and feeling various body parts.

These final two mindfulness practices are more subtle and can prove to be challenging. Practice staying focused, yet patient with your wandering mind or fidgety body. Strike a balance between being disciplined in the practice, yet gentle with your inner voice.

Internal Awareness

This practice of paying attention internally can help you:

- Cultivate acceptance of present moment circumstances as reality.

- Allow for greater focus, clarity, and decision-making.

- Develop awareness of the physical body, energy level, emotions/mood, and mental chatter to catch certain qualities when they are small and choose to take action to rebalance; for instance, noticing the emotion of frustration and choosing to do something to diffuse it before it grows into anger.

The practice of internal awareness can be done independently or to initiate another mindfulness technique. It is simple, but it can be challenging to practice because it involves taking an honest look at what's going on in the dark recesses of your body, your emotions, and your mind. Sometimes, this is not pleasant to do. Sometimes, we might want to judge ourselves for feeling a certain way, having a certain thought, or even for experiencing certain physical sensations.

Following these steps will help you notice what's

happening inside and allow it to be there exactly as it is, without judgment. It's about learning to observe yourself from the outside, as a scientist would, by simply and dispassionately noting what is present.

1. Sit comfortably and either close your eyes or turn your gaze downward.

2. Bring your attention to your physical body. Notice physical sensations, particularly any that feel distracting, like tension in the shoulders or jaw, sensations of soreness or injury. Try not to be reactive to these sensations, but just observe them.

3. If possible, soften around the sensations, letting go of mental resistance to what is present.

4. Now, notice your energy level. In other words, are you tired, wide awake, or somewhere in between? Let go of judgment and story; just notice.

5. Notice your mood and emotions. Is there an underlying emotion present? Allow it to be there and acknowledge it without judging yourself. Notice if there are sensations in the body that are connected to this emotion.

6. If possible, soften any resistance to this emotion.

7. Notice what's going on in your mind. Are your

thoughts taking you to something that's already happened? To ideas or stories about the future? To your to-do list? Try to unhook yourself from being in the center of your thoughts and see if you can observe them, almost as if from the outside. Then, practice letting them float by.

8. From here, you can create a focus anchor, a place to rest your attention. This might be the experience of feeling your feet on the floor, or the contact between your body and the chair or cushion. Keep returning to that simple sensation, and as your mind wanders, curiously make note of it, then return to explore the sensation again and again.

Breath Awareness

In this practice, you are paying attention to your body's natural breathing process, focusing on sensations related to the breath. This practice:

- Cultivates focus and attention.

- Creates clarity and calms the mind with practice.

- Builds self-awareness, emotional regulation, and self-confidence.

- Builds patience and trust in self.

- Improves neural activity and increases gray matter in the prefrontal cortex, our executive functioning / impulse control center.

- Strengthens neural activity in the hippocampus and other memory and recall centers of the brain.

- Reduces activity and activation of the amygdala, the brain's stress center.

Breath awareness, called *anapanasati* in the Buddhist tradition, can be a very challenging practice because it is about letting go of control. The breath is a system that is both automatic and controllable. You can change your breath, breathe in certain patterns, hold your breath, and more. Because your brain knows this and likes order and control, it will attempt to control the natural breath. That is not the point of this practice. The point is to trust your body to breathe all on its own and simply bear witness to it. Feel the sensations associated with your breath. Your mind will wander, and it's your job to redirect it back to feeling sensations of the breath while letting go of the urge to change or control the breath, again and again.

1. Sit in a comfortable position and try to relax.

2. Choose a focal point for breath awareness. Either:

   a. Feel the flow of air in and out at the nostrils

   b. Feel the movement of your chest,

ribcage, or belly

3. Notice the sensations of breath elsewhere in your body (wherever you feel it the most is where you should focus your attention).

4. Wherever you feel your breath the most is where you should focus your attention. That point is your anchor. Return your attention to feel the sensations of one breath at a time. One inhale and one exhale. And then another. Keep going.

5. If you find you're controlling your breathing, intentionally take a deep breath and begin again.

6. Practice for 3-5 minutes to start and work your way up to 10 minutes or more.

7. Be patient with yourself. Be gentle when calling your attention back.

No matter which of these four practices you try, you might feel defeated or say to yourself, *I can't do mindfulness, my mind is too busy.* You are not alone. Most people have this experience in the beginning. You are learning a new way of connecting to and understanding your mind and emotions. It is the same as if you were learning to play an instrument or sport for the first time. It would feel challenging and overwhelming, and you might doubt your ability to succeed. Rest assured that you *can* change the way your mind works. Not only have I seen it in countless clients and students, but I also have personal experience. In addition, there's an abundance of studies on neuroplasticity, mindfulness, and cognitive behavioral therapy, all of which confirm the ability of our brains and our mental-emotional habits to change. It doesn't mean it's easy. It isn't. It takes effort and practice. But as our minds grow sluggish from overusing technology, training our brains to focus has become crucial. When we practice mindfulness, we build cognitive capacity by focusing on one thing at a time: one breath at a time, one body part at a time, or sometimes one repeated word or phrase at a time. This practice of repetition helps teach the brain to focus. We don't have the same focus or patience for lengthy texts as we once did. As I mentioned before, adult literacy rates have declined in the last ten years. Many of us now consume only bite-sized content via social media reels or book summaries.

When we practice mindfulness, we are also training our nervous system to liberate itself from the state of fight, flight, or freeze, where many of us chronically live, just trying to survive. Ask yourself, are you frequently irritated, upset, angry, or feel like people are insulting you or emotionally attacking you? Chances are, the world is not against you, but you are living in your amygdala (the part of the brain wired to scan your environment for danger), and you are *perceiving* that there's an emergency around every corner. Developing a regular practice of mindfulness is the start of deep internal work that can radically change your experience. And this is work that only you can do.

When you cultivate a daily mindfulness practice—even just five minutes—you'll find it becomes easier to stay mindful throughout the rest of your day. You'll grow more aware of your internal state: mind, emotions, and body, in all kinds of life circumstances. You'll notice your jaw tighten when you're talking to your boss; you'll become aware of the increase in self-doubting mental chatter when you're around someone you feel intimidated by; you'll feel deep relaxation in your whole body at the end of a yoga class, or when you're lying in a hammock under your favorite tree. With all this awareness, you'll be able to choose more skillful responses to the stressful moments, and savor the sweet moments more fully, simply because you are in training to slow down, be patient, and practice being a non-judgmental observer of yourself, your environment, and your circumstances. Ultimately, this can help you become more intentional in how you live. Being mindful in everyday life also allows you to notice similar states in others that you've seen in yourself. And if you've learned how to observe yourself with compassion, you will start to extend that compassion to others, recognizing that the challenges of the human condition affect us all. This is how you regulate your reactions. And it's this kind of understanding that strengthens human connection, empathy, and ultimately, emotional intelligence overall. And it can't happen if your nose is in your phone for six or more hours a day, and if it never leaves your palm—that's being connected to technology, not humanity.

When we over-rely on technology to create a sense of connection, we can lose empathy because everything changes behind the screen. Social media isolates us by categorizing us according to our hobbies, interests, spiritual alignment, and political affiliation. It becomes easier to see our differences and forget our similarities, in part because AI algorithms feed us more of what they think we like, and create negative content to reinforce what they think we don't. This process can be so contrived that we might not even know anymore what is actually important to us, which leads us to our next antidote.

Antidote #3: Master Your Values

Many people don't think about their values until they're forced to make a difficult choice, due to a personal crisis or moral dilemma. However, it is empowering and confidence-building to explore and develop your own personal code, so that when challenges arrive, you don't feel lost, but instead you can point to your own internal compass and *know* your path forward.

When you're working toward developing your own moral code, you might explore your spirituality, or perhaps the religion you grew up with. As you look at the "rules" of any structured religion or life philosophy (sometimes it's helpful to explore many), you might ask yourself what resonates with you. Many precepts might seem obvious, "thou shalt not kill," but I'm asking you to investigate these concepts at a deeper level for yourself. For instance, in yogic philosophy, there's a Sanskrit term called *ahimsa*, which is loosely defined as "do no harm."

Using ahimsa or "thou shalt not kill" as an example, explore your thoughts around what this means to you, considering possible moral dilemmas that could arise. For instance, what does it mean for you not to cause harm to anyone? Who does that include: people, animals, bugs? Is it just about killing, or does it include causing other kinds of physical, mental, or emotional harm? What if someone was harming a child, perhaps your child? Would your morals allow you to exert physical force for protection? What if someone broke into your home and was threatening you and your family?

There are no right or wrong answers here. It is not about what other people think. What is important is that you understand what feels right in these kinds of unexpected circumstances, so you can live with yourself and your choices, feeling that you stood by your moral code. Still contemplating the idea of "thou shalt not kill," you might say you're striving toward *causing no harm*, but that you choose to eat meat (killing animals). Or you might say that if someone were hurting your child or threatening their life, you'd make an exception to your moral code. It's not hypocritical; it's an exception to your rule. Once again, you simply need to take some time exploring these kinds of ideas before they happen, so that you're not frozen in the face of such a dilemma.

I suggest reading wisdom texts or even looking at summaries of them (if you're struggling to focus on deep, lengthy writings). Wisdom texts are The Bible, The Bhagahvad Gita, The Yoga Sutras, The Torah, Stoic philosophy texts, and others along these lines.

These ancient writings have guided individuals to find a moral path for thousands of years. One of them isn't necessarily better than another; it's about finding what resonates with *you*. Which one, or which concepts from several, resonate with you the most?

From these, take the time to write out who you want to be and what values are most important to you. Try your best to practice them every day, not just when others are looking, but when you're interacting with wait staff, the janitor in your building, or a random person on the street who catches your eye. In addition, be sure to follow your moral code when engaging with technology.

I will share my moral code here, only so you can see an example, and get started on your own. It's not something to turn over to ChatGPT. This needs to come from deep inside you.

My moral code (and how I define and apply these concepts) is as follows:

- Connection:
    - I will connect with myself through meditation and exploration of spirituality by regularly reading wisdom texts and keeping meaningful quotes nearby so I can remember them, and practice applying them to my daily life. I will connect with others in my life in person as much as possible, doing all I can to create deep, meaningful relationships by listening

to others and being present with them.

- Care:
  - I will care for my body as it is my temple by eating healthfully, exercising, meditating, and taking time for myself and my needs. I will care gently for those I love in the ways they need me to.
- Kindness:
  - I will practice kindness and compassion towards myself when I misstep. I will be kind towards others, under the positive assumption that everyone is trying their best. I will try not to cause physical, emotional, or mental harm to others. Exclusions include dire circumstances where my life or the life of my loved ones is threatened.
- Composure:
  - I will practice ease and letting go, trying not to sweat the small stuff. I will be a dependable, solid friend, partner, therapist, teacher, and mentor. I will hold space for any challenging circumstance with calm, open composure.
- Skillfulness:
  - I will utilize my practice of mindfulness and choose the best course of action as I can, moment to moment. I will be honest in all

circumstances, tempering it with kindness. I will continually try to communicate clearly and succinctly. I will listen to others closely, with full attention.

- Growth:
  - I will continue on a path of learning and will always try to be a better version of myself tomorrow than I am today, while still accepting myself in each moment as a flawed human with the best of intentions. I will practice all these qualities listed here with focus and gentle determination.

- Patience:
  - I will practice remembering that circumstances unfold in time, not on my schedule. Faster is NOT always better. I will be patient with myself when I make mistakes. I will sit with impatience, hold it gently, and breathe until the tension passes.

- Trust:
  - I will surrender when I feel resistance, so I don't end up metaphorically beating my head against a wall. I will instead try to find the lesson in every circumstance under the positive assumption that it is happening for a reason. I will try to cultivate trust that all will be as it should be.

To be clear, the point of having a moral code is not so you beat yourself up when you fall short of its perfect application. It serves as a guide and a reminder of who you are and how you want to present yourself in the world. When you fall short (because we all will fall short sometimes), try to simply shrug your shoulders and say, *It's okay, I'll try again tomorrow.*

This is how you build character and develop your own personal identity. It's not about others' perception of you or what you "should" be. It's about what makes you internally say, *Yes. This is me. This is who I am at my best, in my own skin, in my own heart, in my own mind.* You'll create purpose and meaning daily because you have a guide to handle whatever comes your way. Your actions will be guided by your virtues.

As you become more aware of your values, take time to reflect on how AI and technology shape how you live them. Consider creating a personal guide to help you use technology mindfully, and eventually discuss or establish shared tech boundaries with your family or organization. *The AI Antidote* is ultimately about helping you define those personal and collective boundaries between your humanity and technology. I'm not suggesting we reject technology or deny its potential value, but rather that we approach it with care and intention. Deciding how you'll engage with it deserves more than a passing thought. In the conclusion of this book, I'll offer a framework to help you design your own thoughtful approach to using AI.

Mastering your values, finding your deepest, best self, what is most important to you, and living from that place every day is perhaps the most essential AI antidote. Artificial intelligence can't compete with it.

Antidote #4: Prioritize People

As you do your internal work and learn more about yourself, what you believe, and how you want to show up in the world, you'll see that we don't, and can't, live in a vacuum. We are, in fact, tribal by nature. All the mindful awareness of yourself, your tendencies, your morals, and your values, doesn't matter without the application of this internal work towards human interactions and relationships. And that's hard to do behind a screen.

Human beings learn about relationships as babies. Before we develop language skills, we observe interactions and develop an understanding of social dynamics, gain expectations of how relationships function, and learn how to behave. We mimic what we've learned by watching our family and through our early friendships on the playground. If you have children, perhaps you've observed this. But with more and more adults spending so much free time scrolling on their phones, what are children observing? Have you noticed couples and even families out at restaurants where everyone sits around the table in silence, staring at the screens in their palms? Is it any wonder babies and toddlers reach for technological devices? It's what they observe. It's how they think *things are*. They aren't learning much about body language, facial expression, making eye contact, establishing connections, or problem-solving. These social skills used to be learned on the playground by trial and error and at home through interactions with siblings and parents. But today, parents and kids are spending between seven and nine hours in front of screens each day. This is not prioritizing people.

Given that so many people spend significant time on their devices each day, we need to examine the relational behavioral patterns that have been created and normalized over the past ten years.

Anything But Face-To-Face

The trend toward online connection began before the COVID-19 pandemic. It started by sharing with "friends" on social media, such as Facebook and Instagram, and extended to Zoom work meetings with employees scattered across distances. These technologies initially offered a method of feeling like you're *there* with people who are far away; distance collapsed, and we felt closer. However, the unintended consequence, after years of living with these platforms, is that life has become "performative." Rather than simply being present with a person or group, individuals now devote much time and effort to curating their social media profile and image to fit how they want to be perceived. This is often due to unspoken pressure to connect with more people, more frequently, and across even greater distances, thereby making interactions more about quantity than quality. If we have thousands of "friends" or "followers," maybe we won't feel lonely anymore, or at least we won't look like we are lonely.

In some ways, the distance that online connections create is comforting, because we can choose to show only the good parts of our lives and our personalities. We don't have to let people in to see us at our most vulnerable. In a Zoom meeting, it's easier to sit with your camera off than to be fully present in a room with colleagues. This easy "out" prevents us from building the resilience and social skills needed for true, authentic connection. It's also easier and faster to text or email than to communicate in person or by phone. However, in digital interactions, you lose the subtle cues that are essential to human connection. These critical cues include body language, facial expressions, scent, the shared physical space, the unconscious rhythm of a conversation, and the feeling of someone's energy. Communicating without non-verbal cues forces us to fill in the blanks, and this can lead to misunderstandings, anxiety, and a sense of emotional distance, even when the wording is technically "clear." If most of your interactions are via a digital platform, you might feel more alone than ever, because there's less depth and quality to online relationships. This phenomenon could partially explain the parallel increase in loneliness, anxiety, and depression in the last five years. As these methods of connection have grown exponentially, they have substantially replaced higher-quality in-person, face-to-face interactions.

Yet we are still surrounded by people: the cashier in the grocery store (if you use that aisle instead of self-checkout), the server in the restaurant, the barista at the coffee shop, the other people at the bar or tea shop. Do you acknowledge these human beings? Do you make eye contact and interact with them?

Being human-centered means that we need to look up from our phones, create a renaissance of in-person connecting, and renew the capacity to manage real relationships. I believe this is already happening. People are starting to realize how skillfully AI is creating social media posts so convincing that the lines between reality and fantasy are becoming increasingly blurred. It's hard to know if what you're seeing is real or something created for entertainment or persuasion. We need to return to the messiness of human connection and learn how to cope with it. It's messy because people are flawed, even when we are trying our best. We have opinions, emotions, and experiences. We are not perfect or even necessarily skilled communicators, and we don't always do the right thing, even if we have the best of intentions. Dealing with other humans is hard! You need to be patient, forgiving, and committed to working through difficult interactions and experiences. You need to remember, or learn for the first time, that other people have feelings just like you, and you can't just click a button or "swipe left" to make them *go away* any time you disagree or get annoyed.

When most of our interactions take place behind a screen, it's easy to disconnect from the fact that there's a person on the other side of the interaction, because you don't see their face, their body language, or even hear their immediate response. You get used to being unfiltered with your communication. But think about what unfiltered means. It means you're dumping your dirty sediment on someone instead of filtering it to make it clearer, kinder, and more concise, while still being honest. Yes, it takes effort to communicate clearly, kindly, concisely, and honestly. Effort is a required component of human relationships, whereas with technology, or if you're talking with an AI chatbot, you can do and say whatever you want because it's there to serve you. With AI, your growth in emotional intelligence takes a back seat to a self-centered perspective and behavior... which leads me to another element of how to prioritize people.

The Courage to Disagree,
The Commitment to Understand

Over the last several years in the United States, people have been exceptionally divisive in their rhetoric and their actions, particularly online. I have known many people who sever ties with friends, family, or anyone who doesn't share the exact same opinion they do.

The cost of this division is stress, broken relationships, and stagnation in resolving issues. Regardless of what the disagreements are about, this cycle of division creates feelings of pressure, resistance, and often loneliness.

Staying in a conversation or relationship when you disagree requires courage. You must be willing to honestly *try* to see someone else's perspective and face your own righteousness with curiosity. The Shambhala tradition,[36] encourages this kind of radical curiosity and suggests staying open to listen to and understand another person's perspective. Allowing yourself to metaphorically walk in another human being's shoes cultivates compassion and connection. Of course, there is a difference between tolerance (putting up with someone) and understanding (making a genuine effort to see their view). It is not easy, especially if you are firmly attached to your way of seeing things. Consider listening and responding as if you are genuinely trying to understand the other person's view, instead of having your own validated. If you are willing to attempt this kind of courage, you'll be a leader of change in a polarized world.

In a recent New York Times article, "In the Age of AI, Major in Being Human," David Brooks stresses the importance of college students studying subjects that strengthen human skills. He tells them, "If you can understand another person's perspective, you have a more valuable skill than the skill possessed by some machine vacuuming up vast masses of data about no one in particular."[37]

Prioritizing human relationships requires strength. People are mentally and emotionally messy, but also creative, warm, smart, and capable of friendship, loyalty, and deep connection. If you want to experience significant growth and learn to see the best in people, surround yourself (at least sometimes) with people who disagree with you. Let go of the need to be constantly validated and learn to listen, rephrase, and respond skillfully and diplomatically. And don't let different points of view impact your confidence. We don't all have to agree. We also don't all have to be best friends. Finding a middle ground involves skillfully prioritizing human beings over the unchallenging algorithms AI might feed you. In the next chapter, you'll learn strategies and contemplate a mindset for bravely allowing everyone to express their views without letting things devolve into bickering or bashing.

Before we explore how to lead with curiosity, these suggestions may help you prioritize people in your life:

- Don't treat people as if they were only a function of their roles or jobs. Remember, they are human too, struggling with their own challenges, and celebrating their own little victories. Do you want to be a light in their day, or someone who ruins it?

- Engage with people in your community by simply saying hello and checking in with your neighbors, the cashier, and the people who frequent the same places you do. You don't have to make them your best friends; just ask them how their day is going and wish them well.

- Be friendly and kind, not only because it will make someone else's day, but because *you* will feel better too.

- If you don't already gather with friends or family regularly in person, start a new tradition: a game night, potluck, or book club. Feel like you don't have enough people to form a group? Invite co-workers or neighbors, or even that barista who made your coffee. People are longing for connection.

- Make time for people in your life who are struggling. Sometimes we don't know what to say when someone is grieving, when they've lost their job, when their spouse walks out, when they get sick, so we text, "Let me know if you need anything." Then we distract ourselves from feeling uncomfortable. Your loved ones aren't looking for the perfect words; there aren't any. What they will appreciate is your presence. Your homemade soup. A hug. They probably want space to feel seen, heard, and cared for. That's something that only human connection can provide.

This is how you prioritize people over machines. You remember how we are all similar, and you get curious about the rest.

Antidote #5: Lead with Curiosity

One of my favorite television series of all time is Ted Lasso. Ted is an unassuming man who becomes the head coach of a Premier League soccer team in England. In Season One, episode 8, Ted famously and unexpectedly beats rude, judgmental Rupert in a high-stakes game of darts. Just before he throws the winning bullseye, he tells a touching story, the end of which he recounts a quote attributed to Walt Whitman, "Be curious, not judgmental."[38] Rupert never expected Ted to win, because he made a lot of negative assumptions about him that were based on where he was from and his gentle personality. Had Rupert been curious and asked Ted some pointed questions before betting on the game, he might not have lost.

Some of our autopilot judgments are so deeply ingrained that we might not be conscious of them. In many ways, judgment is how our brain quickly sums up the circumstances (and people) in front of us. Not all such judgments are bad. Some generalizations help us understand people better, and there might be some accuracy in certain common judgments. However, if we operate only on autopilot, we risk missing important information about individuals— like key personality components or belief systems. Such oversights can lead to misunderstanding a person's actions. You can't think that you have all the answers; you must be open to being curious about what you don't know.

Fortunately, we have collective wisdom gleaned from across cultures to remind us that autopilot judgment is not helpful. Here are a few quotes to help us remember the problems inherent in judging others:

> "Why do you look at the speck of sawdust in your brother's eye and pay no attention to the plank in your own eye?" ~ Matthew 7:3-5

> "Remember that your perception of the world is a reflection of your state of consciousness." ~ Eckhart Tolle[39]

> "Before you start pointing fingers, make sure your hands are clean." ~ (widely attributed to) Bob Marley

Finally, the Zen Buddhist teacher Thich Nhat Hanh discusses the idea of judgment in the context of knowledge and understanding. He tells us,

> In Buddhism, knowledge is regarded as an obstacle to understanding, like a block of ice that obstructs water from flowing. It is said

that if we take one thing to be the truth and cling to it, even if truth itself comes in person and knocks at our door, we won't open it. For things to reveal themselves to us, we need to be ready to abandon our views about them.[40]

In other words, we need to open ourselves to curiosity.

Curiosity is one of the purest forms of leadership. This isn't leadership that depends on a title or a team, but the kind sparked by curiosity—the kind that shifts a conversation, softens a disagreement, or opens space for someone to share more of themselves. When you lead with curiosity, you signal openness instead of defensiveness, presence instead of pretense. In a world that moves too quickly and rewards quick conclusions, curiosity slows us down long enough to ask, *What else might be true here?*

To ask this question, you must be prepared to question your assumptions.

Loosen Your Grip

You don't need to feel bad for having your own viewpoint, nor should you abandon all your opinions entirely. Having a personal view is part of being human, and points of view often align with values and morals. The key is to become aware when you are seeing a situation so narrowly that it creates tension in a conversation, interaction, or relationship. This is an indication that you are tightly clinging to "only one way" of being. You might then say to yourself inside your own mind, *Ah, here I am just seeing things from my own perspective.* You don't have to judge yourself for judging, just notice it. In that moment of awareness, you might be able to choose curiosity instead of unexamined judgment.

The shift from a narrow view to open curiosity can be challenging, but the benefits are worth the effort. Now, when you communicate, you'll be shifting the goal from "winning" a discussion to genuinely understanding someone else's view. This practice of curiosity over certainty creates the idea of a perspective gap; there's a difference between what you believe and what the other person believes. Personal history, fear, and values lie within that gap. Good, curious questions bridge that gap and create understanding.

Make Peace your Goal

If you're not sure how to get started, you could simply say, "Hmm, that's interesting. Tell me more." Or ask how they arrived at the conclusion they did, and keep asking them to tell you more, or say, "How come? Or why is that?" Using open-ended questions that can't be answered with a simple yes or no gives others the space to share their thoughts and beliefs. You could be more specific, depending on the circumstances, but filter the inquiry through a lens of genuine interest in understanding, rather than persuasion toward your opinion. No matter the topic or relationship, when you lead with curiosity, people will appreciate you as a communicator, you'll gain a whole lot more empathy and understanding for people, and you will honestly learn a lot. Perhaps you'll maintain your original viewpoint, and that's okay, but hopefully it will have broadened just a little due to sincere curiosity.

Ultimately, the goal should be peaceful coexistence, rather than agreement. We shouldn't all have to think the same, feel the same, or have the same opinions. If we aren't directly harming someone with our actions, we should be able to think and believe what we want. This is vital within families, communities, and in the workplace. Respecting others' ideas is a skill that has been lost amid the widespread use of AI-driven social media platforms that encourage division rather than peaceful acceptance of differences.

Separate the Person from their Position

We've also lost the practice of how to skillfully separate what we like about someone from what we don't. For instance, you can love your goofy Uncle Bob for his sense of humor and kindness, but completely disagree with his politics. You can admire your colleague's work ethic, but disagree with his weekend partying. You can love your best friend because you're so in sync, but you can dislike her choice of a husband. Human beings are complicated. You are complicated. We all seek to be loved and accepted for who we are, as we are, with our positive traits, mistakes, opinions, and choices. No one is perfect. And no one is going to be exactly like you. That is okay. You can love them anyway. Or sometimes you might choose to love them from afar. But tossing out a whole relationship because of someone's stance on one thing can lead you on a path of isolation and loneliness, because you'll likely run out of people who are exactly like you.

Separating the person from their position, ideology, or beliefs means that you can practice noticing all the things you like about someone. You can also notice things you don't like about them. But you don't have to fix anything, change your entire view of the person, or love them less. Let the person be complicated. Let them have their human experience, and the lessons that come with it. Allowing them to be who they are doesn't have to affect or offend you. By no means am I advocating for you to be in relationship with a person who is abusive in any way. But consider if you feel "abused" simply because someone disagrees with you. Is there a way you could get curious about their position, and consider their history, youth, and other belief-shaping experiences?

The practices of prioritizing people and leading with curiosity go hand in hand. Both practices share the perspective that people are complicated, generally not all good or not all bad, but nuanced, interesting, and inconsistent. You can choose to focus on what you enjoy about someone and let their quirks fade into the background. You may choose to practice skillfully communicating with them to understand their perspective, or you may stick to topics that are easier for both of you to enjoy. Remember, you don't have to express every thought in your head. Choosing to value the relationship and peaceful coexistence is remembering that we are all a part of messy humanity. And peace doesn't come from anger, pressure, arguments, judgments, harsh words, or avoidance. Peace comes from practicing empathy, curiosity, and kindness. Cultivating peace isn't easy, but it's worth striving for.

Antidote #6: Choose the Struggle

Michael Easter's *The Comfort Crisis* illustrates what happens when life becomes too easy: we atrophy. When human beings avoid challenge and cling to comfort, we lose our adaptability, resilience, and confidence in our own ability to solve problems. Technology feeds this tendency. It offers a friction-free existence where AI chatbots validate our every thought, games and social media keep us endlessly soothed, and algorithms deliver a steady stream of gratification. We begin to confuse stimulation with satisfaction and ease with well-being.

But the very discomfort we work so hard to avoid is what makes us human. Real-world struggle — whether it's a difficult conversation, a creative block, or a physical challenge — strengthens us. It builds endurance, empathy, and self-efficacy. Of course, when life feels heavy or uncertain, the impulse to retreat into convenience is strong. Doubt whispers, *what if I can't do it? What if I fail or look foolish?* Comfort seduces us with a promise of safety.

Yet on the other side of struggle lies something comfort can never give us: growth. The moment we push through difficulty or solve a complex problem, we experience satisfaction, meaning, and purpose— even when it isn't perfect. This forward motion, this transformation through adversity, reflects what psychologists call post-traumatic growth (PTG). We talk a lot about post-traumatic stress disorder (PTSD) , the pain that follows hardship, but not enough about PTG, the expansion that happens because of it.

Perhaps you recall the story of Malala Yousafzai, a 15-year-old girl from Pakistan who was shot in the head by the Taliban on her way to school because she spoke out against their efforts to prevent girls from attending school. Malala survived the attack, worked hard to recover from her injury, and, undeterred by the intimidation and violence she faced, continued her advocacy work. Two years later, in 2014, she became the youngest recipient of the Nobel Peace Prize. Malala is an excellent example of PTG. She faced an extreme struggle on multiple fronts and grew through the whole experience.

I could continue sharing stories of exemplary people who have overcome and grown from tragic circumstances, but it's more important to ask you to reflect on what you have overcome in your own life. Your story doesn't have to match or exceed someone else's because the point is to be aware of how you've grown through a difficult situation. I know I experienced a tremendous amount of growth as a single mom and homeowner, putting myself through graduate school while barely making ends meet. That uncomfortable time in my life taught me that I was mentally, emotionally, and physically stronger than I realized. It gave me the confidence to move forward with less fear in future endeavors.

Life has gotten much easier for me in many ways, yet I try not to let myself get too comfortable. Many in the Western world are so comfortable that we can't tolerate mild to moderate shifts in the weather, let alone real hardship. Most of you probably have enough food to eat every day and an adequate, climate-controlled home. Perhaps one of your most stressful events is when Wi-Fi goes out or you drop your cell phone and it breaks.

I'm not suggesting that you surrender your modern conveniences forever, but taking a break from them can give you an intentional opportunity for growth. Consider activities like camping, fasting, a physical challenge such as a 5K walk or run, a tech-free week, or participating in a mild-exposure challenge (a social activity if you're shy). You'll be "choosing the struggle," and in turn building your capacity to get comfortable being uncomfortable; that is, assuming you don't complain incessantly and allow yourself to become miserable. It's fine to acknowledge your struggle in a new or difficult circumstance, but the idea is to cultivate the belief that we can work through difficulties with composure, no matter what. Equanimity only comes with practice, so try not to criticize yourself if you complain your way through your first intentional struggle activity. Remember that you are building your capacity for coping with challenges every time you make it through an uncomfortable circumstance.

However, even a very comfortable life contains certain uncomfortable realities. In the West, we tend to brush off certain facts of life because we are so focused on resisting them. We don't want to age, so we have anti-aging products. Some people, including myself, are health nuts, thinking we can ward off every single illness or ailment by eating healthy food. We live as if death will never arrive at our door. And we feel shocked when our lives or relationships change.

The Five Remembrances is a valuable Buddhist teaching that encourages us to face the realities of being human. They are:

1. I am of the nature to grow old. There is no way to escape growing old.

2. I am of the nature to have ill health. There is no way to escape ill health.

3. I am of the nature to die. There is no way to escape death.

4. All that is dear to me and everyone I love is of the nature to change. There is no way to escape being separated from them.

5. My actions are my only true belongings. I cannot escape the consequences of my actions. My actions are the ground upon which I stand.

In other words, we must accept that these facts of life are beyond our control and learn to manage the challenging emotions that accompany them. I recommend sitting with each of the remembrances and noticing any internal resistance. I realize that they sound grim and perhaps even overwhelming. However, there's a valuable growth opportunity in each one. For example, I always thought I'd skip the second remembrance, "I am of the nature to have ill health." As a lifelong healthy eater, exerciser, and meditator, I always felt confident in my ability to be healthy and strong. That is, until I wound up in the emergency room at age 42 with a pain in my chest.

"We found that you have an elevated enzyme in your blood that could be indicative of a heart attack," said the attending physician calmly.

"No, no, no," I said. "I have perfect cholesterol and low blood pressure; I eat right, exercise, and manage stress. I'm not having a heart issue. I think it's just bronchitis." I didn't want to see reality clearly.

Nevertheless, I had to check into the hospital and undergo an EKG, heart catheterization, and numerous other tests. All the while, I was either in denial or I was furious at my body for betraying me. At one point, I was crying hysterically. Suddenly, I recalled the Five Remembrances. My hysterics immediately stopped. I was able to regain the rational self-control in which I had trained myself. "I am of the nature to have ill health. There is no way to escape ill health." I said it out loud. I realized that whatever the outcome of the tests, I would have to choose the struggle: accept reality as it is and move forward as skillfully as possible. My actions are my only true belongings. In this scenario, I was blessed to recover completely from a case of myocarditis (heart inflammation), and return to my healthy self with full respect for honoring the uncertainty of life.

This was a tremendous growth opportunity, and although I didn't exactly choose it, I did choose to accept it and thereby, learned a great lesson. Cultivating a steady mind and heart through difficult times will help you see life with greater clarity and enable you to brush off the minor inconveniences that arise in everyday life. This clarity, which comes from surviving challenges, can empower you to move forward, moment by moment, with greater resilience, focus, and respect for life. The Stoic philosophers remember this concept with the phrase, *Memento Mori,* or Remember Death. It's not meant to be dark or gloomy, only to remind us that as humans, our lives are limited, and we need to make good decisions. These philosophers ask, "Knowing life is limited, how do you want to be spending your time?"

Will you choose to take your dog on an extra walk, remembering that he will only be around for a fraction of your life? Will you decide to take care of your own health, as best you can, to be as healthy as possible? Will you make an effort to spend time with your parents, knowing they won't always be there, or your own children, because *you* won't always be there? Assess how you're spending your time, because it's all you have.

If you're frequently engaged in a world of technology and AI, where you can drown yourself in distraction and illusion, you might be avoiding these facts of life. Perhaps the limited nature of life brings up such feelings of discomfort that you dive back into a comfortable illusion, like AI videos of cats and dogs doing silly things. While sometimes this might be the only way you can cope, staying there for too long is a detrimental avoidance of your feelings and reality. In this case, elements of technology are robbing you of your valuable time.

But, life will always provide circumstances that bring up these human conditions. You can't avoid them forever. This is where the practice of choosing the struggle helps you. If you can become comfortable with being uncomfortable *before* life throws you something unexpected , you'll move through the situation with greater ease, focus, and skilled action. Situations may still be painful or difficult, but you'll *know* you have the capacity to move through them.

Science backs this up. A region of the brain called the anterior midcingulate cortex (AMC), which is linked to willpower and motivation, grows stronger when we face discomfort and push through it. In other words, your brain doesn't grow through ease; it grows through effort. If you want to be more resilient, focused, and emotionally regulated, challenge yourself. Susan Jeffers coined the phrase "Feel the fear and do it anyway" in her 1987 book of the same name.[41] Although we are sometimes encouraged to do what is easiest, choosing the struggle is imperative for strengthening your brain.

Practice choosing the struggle and strengthening your brain by undertaking a mildly to extensively uncomfortable task from this list:

- Drive without depending on your navigation app, especially in your hometown. If you get lost, try to figure out your way back before opening a maps program.

- Enjoy a whole weekend without technology (turn it completely off or leave it behind).

- Eat a meal in a restaurant alone and don't have your face in your phone. People watch, strike up conversations, feel the discomfort, and survive it.

- Have a long-avoided conversation with a difficult person in your life. Prepare for it. Stay calm.

- Try camping if you haven't done it before, or at least take a long walk in the woods by yourself with your phone off.

- Sign up for and participate in a physical challenge. You don't have to be in peak condition to walk a 5k.

- Travel alone to somewhere you've always wanted to go. Don't overplan; figure it out along the way.

- Care for an elderly dog or cat and be with there when they pass.

- Sit with someone who is dying, be it your loved one, or a stranger, as a volunteer in a hospice.

As you work through some of the items on this list, remember the goal is to practice equanimity amid challenges. Use mindfulness to notice your inner experience. Breathe deeply and use positive self-talk, *I've got this*. As you reflect on your post-experience feelings and growth, remember that they derive from confronting real-life struggles and provide lessons technology can't teach you. You will grow and be a better human being because you embraced the struggle.

Antidote #7: Unplug Daily

By now, you've likely noticed a theme: when our relationship with technology is unchecked, it chips away at our focus, our nervous system, and our sense of connection to ourselves and others. While AI, smartphones, and social platforms offer some useful tools and conveniences, they also demand constant attention, often at the expense of our well-being.

In the last few years, several clients have expressed feeling disconnected from their spouses due to their social media or phone use. One said, "It's always in the palm of his hand, at dinner, when we are watching a show, or taking a walk. I find myself feeling almost jealous of the attention he gives technology."

I've also seen couples with such seemingly unresolvable communication problems that they turn to Chat GPT to "fix" things for them. Ironically, this decision causes them to completely disengage with each other by relegating their tough conversations to a machine. As one client told me,

Every time my wife texts me and seems upset, I just copy and paste her text into the Chat, and whatever it comes up with for a response, I just copy and paste it back and send it to her. Works great, she seems happy, and I don't have to deal with it.

Many people turn to chatbots during sleepless nights and moments of boredom. Some feel withdrawal symptoms if they can't connect with their chatbot or social media for periods of time, like when they're at work. As one client shared, "It makes me feel comfy to check in with my socials and chat with one of my favorite bots. But I started to realize that's all I do these days."

Smartphones, laptops, and constant digital alerts keep our sympathetic nervous system, our fight-or-flight mode, on high alert. Each ping, buzz, or scroll can trigger a subtle stress response, pulling us out of the present moment and into a state of reaction. Over time, this leads to mental fatigue, sleep disturbances, and difficulty regulating emotions. Ironically, the more digitally connected we are, the more disconnected we feel. Ask yourself:

- When is the last time I felt irritability, fatigue, plagued by phone vibrations, or unable to focus?

- When was the last time I went 30 minutes or more without my phone?

- How do I feel when my phone is out of reach?

On the retreats I lead, I encourage participants to be as unplugged as possible for the duration of our time together. While this recommendation is challenging for many, the feedback at the end of the experience is positive:

"I felt free without my phone in my pocket."

"I noticed the sky and the smell of the air."

"I was able to let go of feeling obligated to check my email."

Unplugging isn't a rejection of technology. It's a return to yourself.

Unplugging daily, even for short stretches of time, helps you reset. It gives your mind space to wander, reflect, and simply *be*. And in that *being*, you can authentically connect with those around you, daydream, problem-solve, or just breathe deeply. You can notice the urge to use your device and try to let it go. Start with short periods of time. Whether it's setting your phone aside during meals, turning off notifications after 8 pm, or taking a walk without earbuds, these tiny acts of digital surrender remind your brain it's safe to slow down.

Here are a few ideas to experiment with:

- Turn off all notifications on your phone or smart watch. Only check it during set times, perhaps at the top of each hour.

- If you choose to keep a vibration as a notification signal, pause for one long, slow, deep breath before looking at or responding to it.

- Keep your phone out of reach during conversations, meals, and moments of pause.

- Set a tech curfew (perhaps 9 pm) and use that time to read, stretch, or simply rest.

- Try a silent, tech-free morning; wake up naturally.

- Try a full tech-free day once a week or once a month.

- Take a longer break, perhaps a week each year, where your nervous system can reset away from screens and scrolling.

Unplugging isn't about rigid rules. It's about reclaiming space. You might be surprised how quickly you notice the difference in your sleep, your mood, your clarity, and your sense of presence. Try just one unplugging experiment this week. Notice how you feel when you reconnect with yourself, away from technology.

Antidote #8: Cultivate Creativity

When my husband and I eat out at a restaurant and discover a new favorite dish, I try to deconstruct it by savoring it slowly. I'll make some notes and then try to recreate it at home. My husband is impressed when I'm successfully able to do this. For me, it's a form of play. I'm a foodie, and I've been cooking, from both recipes and my own creations, for 30 years. My hubby, on the other hand, will note a favorite cocktail when we are out, but he will go home and ask ChatGPT to recreate it. I've challenged him and ChatGPT to a creative cocktail remake, and our concoctions come out very similar. I try to use this as an opportunity to convince him to exercise his own creative ability and leave other puzzles to ChatGPT. Why? Because it's not about perfection. It's about curiosity and play.

When was the last time you created something just for the joy of it, not for productivity or perfection, but for the sake of play and self-satisfaction?

Being playful isn't just for kids. For adults, play is a biological catalyst for creativity, well-being, and connection. Research shows that playful activities activate curiosity and divergent thinking, relieve stress by lowering cortisol and boosting mood, and strengthen empathy and social bonds through laughter and cooperation.[42] Adults benefit just as much as children, whether through physical play (sports, dance), social play (games, improv), or creative play (art, writing, tinkering). Unstructured, low-pressure play opens access to what positive psychology calls "flow" states that fuel innovation and boost feel-good brain chemicals, resilience, and joy; play isn't a luxury but an essential practice for mental health and human growth.

To be clear, digital "play," endless scrolling, algorithm-driven gaming, or virtual achievements, mimics the feeling of fun while quietly training the brain for instant gratification. Although it stimulates reward loops that keep us chasing the next dopamine hit, digital play rarely leaves us feeling fulfilled or connected. In contrast, embodied play, activities like making music, dancing, crafting, gardening, cooking, or building something tangible, engages all the senses. This type of play anchors us in the present moment, sparks creativity, and strengthens neural pathways tied to learning, focus, and joy. Digital play numbs; embodied play awakens.

I encourage a playful spirit during the retreats I lead by offering charades, word games, and ecstatic dance as mindful, embodied activities to connect the group. The impact is gratifying to witness. Serious, professional adults smile and laugh like kids again. They learn about each other differently, make inside jokes, and years seem to melt away from their faces. Feelings of spaciousness and lightness arouse creativity within, and the resulting inspiration sometimes carries over into an unexpected journal entry or poem.

Being creative when you're overwhelmed and stressed is challenging. Without mental space, a sense of relaxation, and curiosity, imagination starves. And when imagination starves, the beauty of the human soul, usually expressed through creative endeavors, is diminished. This loss of expressed imagination is problematic because creativity is also linked to problem-solving and synthesis. It's the bridge between intellect and intuition.

Yet as AI becomes faster and more adept at generating creative content, it tempts us to outsource our imagination, whether for work or for our own interests. If we surrender this piece of our humanity, we will be losing a lot more than poetry and art. According to a 2024 research review in the *Journal of Creativity,*

> Cognitive flexibility is fostered through creativity, as it encourages flexible thinking, problem-solving, and the exploration of alternative perspectives. These cognitive processes enhance individuals' resilience, adaptability, and coping skills, thus promoting positive mental health outcomes.[43]

Clearly, we shouldn't be using AI for creative endeavors. Not only does it rob us of the opportunity to explore and flex our own intellect in a unique way, but it also blocks our potential for resilience and self-efficacy.

Creativity doesn't ask for much more than time, openness, and a willingness to play. So why do so many people hold back? Often, it's the inner critic that says, *I'm just not creative.* Somewhere along the way, we confused creativity with talent, or with producing something "good enough" to share. Perfectionism creeps in, telling us not to start unless we can guarantee a flawless result. But creativity isn't about mastery; it's about exploration, messiness, and surprise.

Our fast-paced culture doesn't help. We've been conditioned to value efficiency over curiosity and productivity over presence. When every moment is scheduled, creativity feels indulgent, something we'll get to "when there's time." But that time never comes. We fill it with notifications, deadlines, and digital distractions that keep our minds on high alert. The pace itself becomes a barrier to imagination.

Social media compounds the problem. We scroll through a highlight reel of other people's polished output and start to believe originality belongs only to the gifted few. Algorithms reward sameness and predictability, training us to replicate rather than invent. Over time, the combination of perfectionism, comparison, and overstimulation dulls our curiosity. Yet creativity lives in the slow, unstructured spaces that can't be optimized. It begins when we pause long enough to let our thoughts wander and permit ourselves to play, not for productivity, but for joy.

Here are some tips for inviting play and creativity back into your repertoire:

- Allow yourself some unstructured time and don't fill it. Boredom is creative oxygen!

- Listen to your favorite music and dance around your house.

- Start keeping a journal and write stream-of-consciousness thoughts.

- Create something with your hands: cooking, gardening, drawing, painting, or building.

- Allow space for fun, messiness, and imperfection as part of the process.

- Unplug from technology: Digital silence restores originality. Don't compare yourself.

Finally, reflect on three activities you enjoyed doing as a child. Choose one to revisit this week. Not to master it, but just to feel the experience of it again.

As we celebrate human creativity, it's also worth remembering that artificial intelligence learns by drawing from what humans have already made. Every poem, song, and painting it generates is built from the work of real artists, many of whom never gave permission for their creations to be used. This raises important questions about ownership and integrity, but it also reinforces a simple truth: without human imagination, there would be nothing for the machines to imitate. Our creativity is not just personal expression; it is the source code of culture itself, and it deserves our care and protection.

To create is to reclaim your humanity from the algorithm. It isn't just self-expression; it's self-preservation.

Antidote #9 Bathe in Nature

I offer various stress management practices, such as yoga, journaling, and ecstatic dance, in the multi-session women's programs I facilitate. During one session, I saw a young woman intently studying the schedule at the end of class. She finally came close to me and whispered, "Joni, I don't know if I feel comfortable being naked in the woods."

At first, I was confused. Then I realized I had written "forest bathing" on the schedule for Saturday morning. If you haven't heard of forest bathing, you too might be flustered by the title of this antidote. *Shinrin-yoku*, the Japanese term for immersive, therapeutic time spent in nature, directly translates as forest bathing. It does not involve nudity, nor does it necessarily involve washing yourself in a stream or lake. It is also not about hiking or exercise. Forest bathing is simply being present in nature, present with all your senses, noticing what you can see, smell, hear, touch, and (if you're skilled at differentiating what's poisonous from what's not) taste.

Decades of research show that forest bathing boosts both your immune system and your mental health, reduces stress hormones, and activates your body's relaxation response.[44] These benefits are important because to reclaim the best of humanity, we must learn to slow down and get out of the digital urgency state: our fight-or-flight system is chronically activated because screens, alerts, and constant stimulation mimic an emergency. Additionally, we get caught in an overanalyzing, overdoing mindset that is, quite honestly, machine-like. Human beings come from nature, yet we have grown increasingly detached from it. We spend an average of over six hours per day engaging with technology. In addition, we live indoors in a climate-controlled, LED-lit, screen-abundant, noise-filled, human-made world. We lack a connection to where our food comes from and to which local plants are edible or poisonous. We complain about the weather: the snow, rain, clouds, and storms. Some people have an aversion to nature itself. But by avoiding nature, we deprive ourselves of a natural state of mindfulness, as well as the awe, beauty, metaphor, and meaning the natural world offers.

For most of human history, our survival depended on knowing our environment, which plants could nourish or heal, which seasons signaled change, and when to sow and harvest. Today, many Westerners cannot name the trees on their street or identify a single edible plant. That gap reveals how deeply we've outsourced our knowledge to technology.

Indigenous cultures, by contrast, have sustained an intimate, reciprocal relationship with their ecosystems. Their understanding of the land is relational, spiritual, and sensory, allowing them to remain profoundly *human*. They are attuned participants in the rhythms of life rather than detached observers.

My nephew lived in Peru for one summer and spent a lot of time with shamans and indigenous people. At one point, he contracted a bacterial infection in a wound on his knee. He was worried, but the elder of the group laughed at his concern. He put some ash, herbs, and a leaf on my nephew's knee and wrapped it with woven grass. Within a few days, his knee was completely healed. (I later saw photos of the bacterial infection and was surprised he survived.) I wonder if an AI-assisted physician could have saved his knee so easily.

You don't need to learn how to heal a bacterial infection using what's in your backyard, but you could learn to identify a couple of trees or a poisonous plant in your area. In doing so, you are remembering your connection to the Earth and the environment in which you live. In this way, you are honoring your humanity by being attuned to the rhythms of life in your region, rather than being a detached, oblivious passerby plugged into technology rather than reality.

Living in front of a screen keeps your focus narrow and self-referential; nature widens and expands it. Consider the feelings of awe afforded by nature: seeing the Grand Canyon, the Pacific Ocean, the

Rocky Mountains, the Swiss Alps, or the Sahara for the first time: breathing in the air, taking in the colors and the sounds, being fully alive and embodied in your humanness. The feeling of being small within something vast is corrective to our ego and sense of overstimulation. It expands perspective, increases empathy, and reminds us that we belong to something larger than ourselves. To experience this kind of presence and awe takes practice and an intentional effort to step away from a screen. If you are addicted to seeing a natural wonder only through the camera lens on your phone, consider viewing the natural world with your naked eye. When my husband and I watched a glorious sunset on the Greek island of Santorini recently, I was dismayed to see so many people holding up their phones to record nature's majestic close to the day. While I'm not suggesting you never take a photo of a beautiful scene, I am suggesting you enjoy it with your own eyes and other senses first.

Sensory experiences are important because our relationship with technology is almost entirely cerebral. Nature, however, reawakens the sensory and embodied intelligence that defines our humanity. Experiencing the textures of bark, the scent of rain, or the rhythm of walking can anchor us in the physical present and restore our connection to intuition and instinct. Some part of our ancestral self remembers being one with nature, and it soothes our overstimulated brain.

When nature soothes and slows the nervous system, we learn to notice the deeper threads between nature and life, the metaphors and lessons that are all around us but easy to ignore. While human beings struggle with the concept of change, nature demonstrates the constancy of change: night flows into day, seasons flow from winter to spring to summer to autumn. Observing the cycle of deciduous trees can help us feel better about our own aging process as we watch green leaves change color and gracefully fall from branches. Watching a tiny ant carrying a large morsel of food can remind us of our own life struggles. Feeling the power of a thunderstorm can remind us of our own uncontrolled emotions. Sitting with the sounds, smells, and sights of nature can soften our busy minds and help us see ourselves as a part of the world at large.

What small acts of rewilding might you invite into your routine?

- Consider bathing in nature by simply finding a place to sit outside. You don't have to be deep in the woods; you'll get benefits sitting in your own backyard, looking up at trees, and listening to birds. Work your way up to at least 20 minutes of outdoor time a day, regardless of the season or weather.

- Learn to identify a few plants or trees local to your area.

- Learn the phases of the moon and take the time to look up into the night sky to observe them.

- Take a walk without headphones; listen to the sounds of nature.

- If you're on a hike, enjoying nature, pause before you get out your phone and take a photo. Enjoy the scene with your own eyes first. Pause and breathe. Then, if you still want the image, go ahead and take it.

While you're unplugged in nature, ask yourself:

- What information am I taking in with my senses?

- What is my heart telling me about this experience?

- What is my body telling me while I'm here?

Here's another way of being present in the forest:

Consider focusing on one tree. Observe it from its roots to its top. Get closer. Feel its bark. Notice the shape and texture of its leaves. Lean against it or sit with it. What might this tree tell you if it could speak to you?

If you're not used to being in nature, this will be a new experience, and your senses will have a lot to focus on. Try to relax. We come from nature. We are a part of it, and it is a part of us, no matter how many physical, emotional, or digital walls we construct. Remember, this experience is meant to be an immersive time in nature, so unplug from your device and constant man-made sound. In fact, leave your phone at home, in your car, or at least turn it off while you're in the forest. Journal or contemplate your experience with *shinrin-yoku*. Go outside every day, even if just to look up at the sky and take a few breaths. You might just find that you can hear yourself better in nature.

Antidote #10: Trust Your Gut

There's a kind of knowing that doesn't come from thinking, the quiet pull inside that says *yes*, or the uneasy feeling that whispers *not this way*. Long before data, dashboards, or predictive algorithms, this was how we navigated the world. Intuition helped us sense weather shifts, choose allies, and find our way home.

But somewhere along the path to progress, we began to silence that voice. We replaced inner knowing with analytics, instinct with spreadsheets. The more data we collect, the less we seem to trust ourselves. We've come to believe that if it can't be measured, it can't be real. Yet the truth is, your intuition has been measuring everything all along, through emotion, experience, and the body's subtle signals.

There are several approaches to explain that feeling of knowing in your gut. Consider your subconscious mind, which operates in the background. It has been recording every success and failure, every relationship experience, every detail of every subject that interests you, and anything you find meaningful, and it's been learning patterns. Our minds want to keep the patterns that "work" and make us feel good, and eliminate the patterns that "don't work," or make us feel bad. But we don't have a direct, conscious link to our subconscious mind, and so it just quietly whispers to us. When we hear those little whispers and follow them, things often work out well. When we ignore them, we usually regret it.

The study of epigenetics has shown that we can inherit knowledge, personality traits, and even wisdom from our ancestors. This inherent, subtle knowledge resides in the background of our DNA, operating as intuition. Perhaps these deep-seated links to generational intuition can explain why 2nd, 3rd, or 4th-generation doctors, tailors, or writers might be particularly skilled in their crafts. Some might say they were born into a particular profession or come from a long line of ancestors endowed with a special skill.

There is yet another approach that views intuition as a divine or spiritual connection; it's like receiving quiet messages from beyond.

Regardless of how you understand intuition, you have access to this subconscious wealth of deeply personal data through what we call gut instinct. Only you can access your intuition, and it is far more relevant to your life than anything AI could ever offer. In a world that prizes proof over perception, trusting your gut has become a radical act. However, we must remember that wisdom is encoded within each of us and endeavor to access it, even when others doubt it exists.

AI might process data from billions of information points, but it lacks embodied experience, emotion, and context—the very ingredients that make human intuition reliable. For instance, algorithms cannot replicate the professional intuition that comes from thousands of hours of experience in a particular field. Malcolm Gladwell, in his books *Outliers* and *Blink*, explains that it takes roughly 10,000 hours of exposure to success and failure in a specific subject to develop an instinctive ability to make sound decisions instantly.[45] The idea behind *Blink* explains how physicians can sometimes sense a diagnosis before receiving test results, and an art curator can recognize a forgery before scientific analysis confirms it.

Instinct is both something we are born with and something we cultivate. But if we allow AI to solve our problems and provide our answers, we remove the struggle that deepens understanding. Struggle refines perception. Without it, our capacity for intuition weakens. If our children overuse AI, they may never develop that deeper sense of knowing, either in their work or in their personal lives. AI may reach conclusions faster, but without embodied experience and contextual understanding, it will never attain wisdom, and neither will we, if we continue to push intuition aside.

In my work, I've observed many people who have learned to distrust their intuition. We've been conditioned to seek external validation instead of listening inward, especially in a world that keeps telling us data knows best. Many of my clients tell me their instincts have led them astray in the past. I don't believe our true instincts ever lead us astray. When someone follows an inner voice and things don't work out, it's usually not intuition at all, but anxiety, self-doubt, or another reactive emotion masquerading as instinct.

So how do you know if you're listening to your rambling mind or your wise inner instinct?

You must get quiet.

When you take time for solitude and silence, when you can leave your phone and technology behind, you will hear yourself again. Our minds and hearts can be filled with both external noise and our own internal voice of fear. Many people are flooded with sensory input most of the day, whether from conversations, traffic, music, podcasts, television shows, or video clips on their feeds. Silence might feel uncomfortable because it's unfamiliar. In this uncharted quiet, you might notice what lives in the dark recesses of your mind and heart: traumas you've experienced, pain from harsh words and broken relationships, self-deprecating thoughts from mistakes you've made, all running on a loop in the background; it's a lot to face. Internal noise keeps you stuck and uncertain. This is when you can circle back to Antidote #2, Regulate Your Reactions. When you practice mindfulness and deep breathing, you calm your nervous system and sweep the clutter from your weary mind. It's not a one-and-done event; it's something you must repeat daily. Keeping your mind clear and uncluttered requires ongoing effort. Other tools, like journaling and self-reflection, help you learn to distinguish between noise and inner instincts.

You can also cultivate intuition by strengthening the link between your mind and body. This can happen through mind-body practices like yoga, Qigong, and mindful walks in nature. The goal is to develop awareness. Try simply observing your body's reaction in certain situations, like when you meet someone new or when a challenging circumstance arises. How does your belly feel: tight, tense, upset, or settled and relaxed? What is the state of your neck and shoulders? What else can you perceive within your physical body? Try to make note of whatever you observe and stay curious. Try not to overanalyze, as analysis is the opposite of intuition. And finally, try to be patient and free of expectations. If you are looking for a flashing neon sign, you'll likely be disappointed. Intuition whispers; it doesn't often yell.

Your intuition will grow stronger with stillness and self-trust, not with more information. That's why many of the previous antidotes are necessary, and this one is listed last. Knowing yourself, emotionally regulating, living by your values, unplugging, getting creative and curious, embracing struggle, recognizing that adversity leads to growth, and taking quiet time in nature are all steps toward strengthening your inner wisdom.

Understanding the concept of intuition is one thing; recognizing it is another. Before we dismiss intuitive wisdom as coincidence or chance, it helps to see how it knowing has guided people across different situations.

Recently, a client of mine was late to her session. When she arrived, she had quite an interesting story to share. She missed her usual turn on the drive to my office and felt an unexpected draw to take a different route. When she finally pulled into a parking spot, she briefly checked her phone and saw there was an accident on her usual route that morning. She'll never know whether she "avoided" something or just needed a quieter drive, but she noticed that when she slowed down and listened, her body made the decision before her mind did.

When indigenous healers speak of listening to the land, they are referring to the practice of sensing what plants the body needs before identifying them intellectually. This kind of wisdom, which evolves from generations of close observations and relationships with nature, reflects the idea that intuition is a collective inheritance, not just an individual gift.

I was skeptical about this idea myself until I attended an immersive herbalist retreat last year. During one exercise, we were invited to meditate quietly in a garden, reflecting on the kind of healing we needed, and to let a plant "choose us" rather than deliberately selecting one. At the time, I was struggling with chronic pain and awaiting surgery on both my hip and shoulder. Although I had noticed a bright orange flower on my way in and decided it would be my choice, by the end of the meditation, my attention shifted completely. The only flower I could see was a small, fuzzy, purple one with star-shaped petals. Without hesitation, I chose it. Later, I learned it was a powerful anti-inflammatory used to ease joint pain.

Was it a coincidence, or a more profound inner knowing? Whatever it was, the experience reminded me that intuition is real, alive in the body, and always waiting for us to listen.

Intuition doesn't always arrive as a grand revelation. More often, it speaks in quiet, practical ways: a gentle nudge to call a friend, choose a different route home, or pause before hitting "send." It's that subtle tug you feel when something doesn't sit right, or the warmth of recognition when something does. These small, almost invisible moments of knowing guide us through daily life just as meaningfully as the bigger, more obvious ones.

The more we practice noticing these whispers, the more clearly we hear them. Intuition is not a mystery to solve, but a relationship to rebuild, one built on attention, self-trust, and the willingness to listen even when logic wants to take over.

And perhaps that's the deeper message of *The AI Antidote*. In a world growing louder, faster, and more artificial by the day, returning to our inner knowing, to our connections with each other, and to our relationship with the living world around us is how we stay human. The antidote isn't about resisting technology, but remembering what it can never replace: our capacity to feel, to sense, to connect, and to know.

Part Three: Reclaiming the Future

Rehumanization: Redefining Success in an AI World

For too long, we've defined progress by what we can produce, automate, or measure. But as artificial intelligence accelerates those capacities beyond human limits, we're faced with a more important question: what does it mean to succeed as a human being in a world where machines can do almost everything we can?

Regardless of the industry you're in, learning to use AI skillfully will be valuable. Those who don't learn to use AI may be out of work or even left behind entirely. Fortunately, there are countless resources available to help you learn the tools of AI. My focus, however, is on something more essential: how to reclaim and maintain your humanity alongside the rise of AI. We must remember that faster isn't always better. Why not seek depth over data, and shift the idea of success from efficiency and optimization toward human values like wisdom, empathy, creativity, and well-being?

According to an article in the *Harvard Gazette*, published in August 2025, stated, "Business leaders have realized that it's relatively easy to get technical expertise in almost anything, but to get people who can understand and get along with one another, that is a challenge."[46] Understanding and getting along with others involves emotional intelligence skills. Learning and practicing self-awareness, self-control, self-motivation, and skillful social interactions are vital pursuits as we move forward in the age of AI. If we want to ensure that humanity flourishes, we need both emotional intelligence skills as well as ethical and mindful productivity that advances us forward with a human-centric focus.

Rehumanization is about prioritizing emotional intelligence, ethical tech design, and mental health as markers of progress and success. The antidotes presented in this book: curiosity, presence, resilience, creativity, and intuition, are not nostalgic ideals but survival skills—rehumanizing skills— for a future where AI has the potential to overshadow every element of our lives and our humanity. How will we choose to respond?

Living the Antidote

Integrating Daily Practices

The AI Antidote is not intended to be just a set of lofty ideals; rather, it is a guide for cultivating practical habits involving critical thinking, emotional intelligence, and human connection. The ten antidotes offer ways to strengthen these important aspects of humanity, all of which risk atrophying without sustained practice in everyday life. As you review the antidotes, I encourage you to choose the ones that feel most challenging. Then prioritize one skilled action in that area and practice it daily or weekly. As you experience the benefits, consider incorporating more skilled actions into your daily life.

Here are some practical ways to begin integrating the ten antidotes into daily life and engage with AI and technology in an ethical and intentional way.

- Morning Mindfulness & Intentional Technology Use: create rituals for starting the day without screens or prompts. Choose one of the following options:

    - Sit quietly without your phone, savoring your coffee or tea, simply gazing out your window for a few minutes.

    - Begin your day with five to ten minutes of 4:8 breathing.

    - Write in your journal upon rising; don't censor yourself, simply write whatever arises in your mind.

- Micro-Moments of Humanity: small acts of empathy, play, gratitude, and creativity throughout the day:

- ○ Ask a stranger or acquaintance how their day is going; try to make a genuine human connection.

- ○ Pause before each meal for a moment of gratitude for all you have in your life.

- ○ Look for opportunities to brainstorm with coworkers, friends, and family members. Resist the urge to Google the answer; instead, be curious and playful.

- ○ Plan time to do something you love away from technology: dance, hike, garden, read a book, or host an in-person party or game night.

- Digital Hygiene: build on "Unplug Daily" and "Choose the Struggle" as ongoing maintenance of emotional balance.

  - ○ Put your technology to bed by a particular time each evening, preferably at least an hour before you go to sleep.

  - ○ Make dinner time a tech-free zone.

  - ○ Make date night a phone-free experience.

  - ○ Challenge yourself with a physical or mental task: sign up for a 5K or commit to starting a DIY project that feels a bit intimidating.

- Embodied Reminders: bring nature, movement, and presence into daily routines

  - Take a daily outdoor walk, even just a brief one, regardless of the weather.

  - Step outside and look up at the sky each morning and evening to observe its color. Take a deep breath before returning indoors.

- Community Reflection: encourage small groups or workplaces to adopt shared "human practices," like tech-free meetings or weekly reflection circles.

  - Consider beginning this conversation with your family and friends before suggesting it to community event planners and your workplace.

As you engage with these practices, you may want to develop your own personal code regarding your relationship with and use of AI. The following section offers a guided process designed to help you clarify how you choose to engage with AI.

Crafting Your Own Ethical AI Principles: A Guided Process

Step 1: Ground in Self-Awareness

- Reflect on what you most value as a human being—qualities like curiosity, compassion, patience, creativity, honesty, or courage.

  - "When I'm at my best, what values am I living out?"

Step 2: Identify Your Relationship with Technology

- Notice when technology supports you and when it distracts, numbs, or replaces something meaningful.

  - "When do I feel more alive or connected because of technology, and when less so?"

Step 3: Define Your Purpose for Using AI

- Clarify the why behind your engagement with AI.

  - "What do I want AI to help me do, and what do I never want to outsource to it?"

Step 4: Translate Values into Principles

- Turn your reflections into short, memorable statements that act as guideposts.

    ○ "I will use AI to enhance my thinking, not replace it."

    ○ "I will pause before prompting."

    ○ "I will protect the space for human connection and creativity."

Step 5: Check for Balance

- Examine whether your principles balance innovation and restraint.

    ○ Does this principle strengthen my humanity?

    ○ Does it ensure integrity, empathy, and self-awareness in how I use technology?

Step 6: Commit and Revisit

- Write your principles down somewhere visible. Revisit them monthly or after significant technological changes. Revise as your understanding evolves.

    ○ "What have I learned from my interactions with AI this month about who I want to be?"

Extending to Family, Community, Organization

Once you have written your personal principles for engaging with AI, invite others in your family, community, or organization to share their principles in pairs or small circles. Keeping in mind that integrating technology more consciously helps to anchor our choices in clear, ethical principles, ask each person to reflect on how their values intersect and diverge. This discussion builds both accountability and community. For groups or organizations that are already actively using AI tools to assist in everything from proposal writing to lesson planning to responding to emails and phone calls, it is important to step back and consider creating a collective code for ethical engagement with AI. Here is an example of a framework for approaching AI with intention and integrity. The principles it espouses can be adapted for individuals, families, communities, and organizations seeking to engage with AI in a conscious and ethical way.

Principles for Intentional AI Use

Technology has the power to either amplify the best of our humanity or quietly diminish it. When used with awareness, artificial intelligence tools can support us while we preserve what is most essential: our capacity for critical thinking, emotional intelligence, and genuine human connection. As a community dedicated to ethical engagement with AI tools, we will endeavor to be guided by the following principles:

1. Activate Human Capital First

Before we create a prompt, we will think. We commit to beginning every AI task with deep, unassisted brainstorming and human introspection. We define the *problem*, the *vision*, and the *desired outcome* using our own intuition, experience, and emotional intelligence before turning to the machine. This initial self-reliance ensures that AI is used to *execute* an already clear human purpose, not to define it.

2. Lead the Co-Creation

We maintain our role as the lead director and conscious editor. AI is a powerful assistant, but humans remain the source of innovation, context, and discernment. We use our emotional intelligence to critique the AI's output, not just for accuracy, but for tone, relevance, and human resonance. We inject our unique voice and ethical sensibility, ensuring the final product is an authentic expression of our own human judgment.

3. Govern with Integrity and Empathy

Every interaction is an act of stewardship. We apply human integrity to ensure transparency about our AI usage, protecting privacy and respecting copyright. We proactively review the work for bias, misstatement, or harm, using our own empathy and fairness to guide the technology. Our human responsibility is to ensure that the tools we use do not diminish the truth or compromise our relationships.

4. Preserve Your Cognitive Edge

We utilize AI to strategically offload only the most routine and time-consuming tasks. We resist the temptation to outsource the critical high-value skills, such as strategic thinking, complex negotiation, or deep emotional connection that define our humanity. We utilize AI for efficiency, freeing up time for creative problem-solving, learning new human skills, and authentic interaction.

5. Prioritize Authentic Human Connection

We recognize that emotional intelligence is a uniquely human capacity, essential for true understanding and community. We commit to using AI as a tool to *support* our positive purpose: to simplify tasks, solve logistical problems, and amplify our creative reach, but never as a substitute for authentic human interaction, empathy, or genuine connection. Our goal is for AI to free up our time and energy, allowing us to dedicate more of our human capital to real-world engagement and serving others face-to-face. As part of this human-centric focus, we commit to limiting the anthropomorphizing of AI; we will remember that AI is skillful at using algorithms to create the illusion of care and compassion, but it is not a living entity. Treating it as such is a projection of our own humanity, which we shall intentionally focus on other humans.

A Call to Collective Action

Whether we realize it or not, how we use technology, both individually and collectively, will define what it means to be human for the next generation. The internet shaped Millennials. Cell phones shaped Gen Z. AI will shape Gen Alpha and beyond. Without clear guidelines or intentions to protect and strengthen our emotional intelligence and human connection, we risk losing not only our sense of agency and self-efficacy but also continuing the current downward trend in mental health.

Our relationship with technology and AI is shaping all of us in ways we often don't notice. Every scroll, search, and shortcut teaches our brains what to value and how to think. If we approach technology without awareness, we begin to adapt to its rhythms instead of our own. Over time, we risk losing our sense of agency, forgetting that we still have the power to choose how we engage. Real freedom comes from using all kinds of technology intentionally, not reflexively. It means pausing long enough to ask whether a tool is serving our growth or quietly steering our attention away from what truly matters.

The same pattern affects our mental and emotional health. When we rely too heavily on AI for connection or validation, our confidence in real human interaction can fade. Emotional intelligence requires presence, empathy, and discomfort, yet digital life offers constant escape from those qualities. Without boundaries or conscious use, we begin to outsource not only our thinking but also our feelings. If we want the next generation to inherit a world in which both humans and technology thrive, we must model a balanced relationship, one that values emotional depth as much as digital skill.

The antidote begins with you, but it does not end there. Each of us has the power to shape the culture around artificial intelligence, to model a way of living that reminds the world what it means to be human. The future is not written in algorithms; it's written in how we choose to live, create, and connect with each other. Let's lead with the most powerful technology we will ever possess—the human heart and mind—and evolve from there.

Notes

Introduction

1. Kemp, S. (2024, January 31). Digital 2024: Global Overview Report — DataReportal – Global Digital Insights. DataReportal – Global Digital Insights. https://datareportal.com/reports/digital-2024-global-overview-report

2. Americans Express Worry Over Personal Safety in Annual Anxiety and Mental Health Poll. (n.d.). https://www.psychiatry.org/news-room/news-releases/annual-anxiety-and-mental-health-poll-2023

3. Sappenfield, O., Alberto, C., Minnaert, J., Donney, J., Lebrun-Harris, L., & Ghandour, R. (2024, October 1). Adolescent Mental and Behavioral Health, 2023. National Survey of Children's Health Data Briefs - NCBI Bookshelf. https://www.ncbi.nlm.nih.gov/books/NBK608531/#:~:text=In%202023%2C%20more%20than%205.3,%2Fconduct%20problems%20(6.3%25).

4. Haidt, Jonathan. (2024). The Anxious Generation: How the Great Rewiring of Childhood Is Causing an Epidemic of Mental Illness. Random House.

5. Six Seconds. (2024b, June 3). State of the heart • Six seconds. https://www.6seconds.org/emotional-intelligence/research/

6. Sato, K. (2024, March 22). Researcher says high screen time is associated with social, emotional problems in children. ABC News. https://www.abc.net.au/news/2024-03-22/research-finds-screen-time-video-games-linked-social-problems/103606100

Part One: The Quiet Crisis

7. Ribeiro, Jair. "These Are the Best Definitions of Artificial Intelligence You Can Read Today. Do you want to understand what A.I. is? Here, you have some excellent definitions to start with." Medium, March 12, 2023. Accessed October 7, 2025. https://medium.com/swlh/these-are-the-best-definitions-of-artificial-intelligence-you-can-read-today-7c53c0e38584

8. Hill, Kashmir, and Dylan Freedman. "Chatbots Can Go Into a Delusional Spiral. Here's How It Happens." https://www.nytimes.com/2025/08/08/technology/ai-chatbots-delusions-chatgpt.html, August 12, 2025. Accessed October 7, 2025. https://www.nytimes.com/2025/08/08/technology/ai-chatbots-delusions-chatgpt.html

9. Ode on a Distant Prospect of Eton College. (2024, June 22). The Poetry Foundation. https://www.poetryfoundation.org/poems/44301/ode-on-a-distant-prospect-of-eton-college

10. Keyes, Daniel. Flowers for Algernon: And Other Stories, Mariner Books Classics,1959.

11. Alok Jha, "Neutrino Researchers Admit Einstein Was Right," The Guardian, February 14, 2018, https://www.theguardian.com/science/2012/jun/08/neutrino-researchers-einstein-right.

12. Frankl, Viktor Emil. Man's Search for Meaning, 1946. http://lifemanagement4filipinos.weebly.com/uploads/1/2/0/6/12062185/mans_search_for_meaning_-_viktor_e._frankl_1.pdf.

13. Nin, Anaïs. The Diary of Anaïs Nin, 1947–1955. HMH, n.d., page 3.

14. Nin, Anaïs. The Diary of Anaïs Nin, 1947–1955. HMH, n.d., page 3

15. While the concept of non-attachment is a core principle of Buddhism, there are threads of this concept woven throughout various religions, including Hinduism, Taoism, Jainism, and Christianity. It is the foundational recognition of impermanence: that all things change, and if we can accept that, we will suffer less.

16. Easter, Michael. The Comfort Crisis: Embrace Discomfort to Reclaim Your Wild, Happy, Healthy Self. Rodale Books, 2021.

17. Loz Blain, "Use It or Lose It: The Human Brain Will Be Reshaped by AI," New Atlas, February 18, 2025, https://newatlas.com/ai-humanoids/use-it-lose-it-ai-critical-thinking/?utm_source=flipboard&utm_content=New Atlas/magazine/New+Atlas:+Emerging+Technology.

18. Goldstein, Dana, "American Children's Reading Skills Reach New Lows," The New York Times, January 29, 2025, https://www.nytimes.com/2025/01/29/us/reading-skills-naep.html?smid=nytcore-ios-share&referringSource=articleShare

19. Salmerón L, Vargas C, Delgado P, Baron N. Relation between digital tool practices in the language arts classroom and reading comprehension scores. Read Writ. 2023;36(1):175-194. doi: 10.1007/s11145-022-10295-1. Epub 2022 May 7. PMID: 35571994; PMCID: PMC9076497.

20. While not specifically about artificial intelligence, this article discusses the not-so-popular idea (supported by data) that technology is NOT helping kids thrive. Jared Cooney Horvath, "The EdTech Revolution Has Failed,"

After Babel (blog), November 12, 2024, https://www.afterbabel.com/p/the-edtech-revolution-has-failed.

21. An eye-opening article I came across while diving into research about the impact of AI.
Joan Westenberg, "The Death of Critical Thinking Will Kill Us Long Before AI.," Westenberg., November 12, 2024, https://www.joanwestenberg.com/the-death-of-critical-thinking-will-kill-us-long-before-ai/.

22. "The Death of Critical Thinking Will Kill Us Long Before AI.," Westenberg., November 12, 2024, https://www.joanwestenberg.com/the-death-of-critical-thinking-will-kill-us-long-before-ai/.

23. By Jonathan Rothwell, "Teens Spend Average of 4.8 Hours on Social Media per Day," Gallup.Com, March 26, 2025, https://news.gallup.com/poll/512576/teens-spend-average-hours-social-media-per-day.aspx.

24. Jamie F Finn, "Loneliness in America: Just the Tip of the Iceberg? — Making Caring Common," Making Caring Common, October 8, 2024, https://mcc.gse.harvard.edu/reports/loneliness-in-america-2024.

25. Miles Klee, "People Are Losing Loved Ones to AI-Fueled Spiritual Fantasies," Rolling Stone, May 5, 2025, https://www.rollingstone.com/culture/culture-features/ai-spiritual-delusions-destroying-human-relationships-1235330175/.

26. "When the 'Person' Abusing Your Child Is a Chatbot: The Tragic Story of Sewell Setzer," n.d., https://www.humanetech.com/podcast/when-the-person-abusing-your-child-is-a-chatbot-the-tragic-story-of-sewell-setzer.

27. Karen Zraick and Sarah Mervosh, "That Sleep Tracker Could Make Your Insomnia Worse," The New York Times, June 17, 2019, https://www.nytimes.com/2019/06/13/health/sleep-tracker-insomnia-orthosomnia.html

Part Two: The Antidote

28. This is an essential documentary to watch if you are curious about AI. Harrs, Tristan; Raskin, Asa, "The A.I. Dilemma." March 9, 2023. Center for Humane Technology. 1 hour, 7 minutes. https://youtu.be/xoVJKj8lcNQ?si=a_QMPx7RkmoeP3Q5

29. This phrase comes from Thich Nhat Hahn's interpretation of the Buddhist Five Remembrances, first published in The Plum Village Chanting Book (Parallax Press, 1991). https://commongroundmeditation.org/teachings/five-remembrances/

30. Victor Tangermann, "Woman Kills Herself After Talking to OpenAI's AI Therapist," Futurism, August 19, 2025, https://futurism.com/woman-suicide-openai-therapist?fbclid=IwY2xjawMdq9ZleHRuA2FlbQIxMQABHgOAJyOvnsSAGICa55Ih0RNqyz8RmV7sk2Gx60SHawsMS1x500cOzW10r6Kl_aem_hLR3vUxJikEuQ9ibQafeqg.

31. Alex Mazzarisi, "The Power of Journaling: What Science Says About the Benefits for Mental Health and Well-Being," Child Mind Institute, March 21, 2025, https://childmind.org/blog/the-power-of-journaling/.

32. Stamford, Joni Michele Staaf. The Space to Choose: A Path to Life Mastery. Healthy Body Peaceful Soul, LLC, 2024.

33. Coby Kozlowski is a speaker, life coach trainer, and contemporary yoga and meditation educator. I know Coby from my studies at Kripalu Center for Yoga and Health, where I heard her say these words to us as she led multiple trainings, offering a constant reminder of acceptance and growth. https://www.cobyk.com/

34. Van Der Kolk, Bessel A. The Body Keeps the Score: Brain, Mind, and Body in the Healing of Trauma. Penguin Books, 2015.

35. Staaf-Sturgill, Joni. or Staaf-Stamford, Joni. Recordings of Guided Body Scans are Available Online if You Search YouTube @Mindfulness with Joni and on the Insight Timer App under Joni Staaf Stamford (formerly Sturgill).

36. This is a great read to learn more about living with a curious, open mind: Trungpa, Chögyam. Shambhala: The Sacred Path of the Warrior. Shambhala Publications, 2009.

37. David Brooks, "Opinion | in the Age of A.I., Major in Being Human," The New York Times, February 4, 2023, https://www.nytimes.com/2023/02/02/opinion/ai-human-education.html?smid=em-share.

38. Ted Lasso, Season 1, Episode 8, "The Diamond Dogs," directed by Declan Lowney, written by Phoebe Walsh, Apple TV+, 2020.

39. Eckhart Tolle, The Power of Now: A Guide to Spiritual Enlightenment (New World Library, 1999).

40. Mitchell Ratner, "Still Water Mindfulness Practice Center," n.d., https://www.stillwatermpc.org/dharma-topics/be-curious-not-judgmental/.

41. Susan J. Jeffers, Feel the Fear and Do It Anyway (Houghton Mifflin Harcourt, 1987).

42. Saya Des Marais, MSW, "The Importance of Play for Adults," Psych Central, November 10, 2022, https://psychcentral.com/blog/the-importance-of-play-for-adults#benefits.

43. Ducel Jean-Berluche, "Creative expression and mental health," Journal of Creativity, Volume 34, Issue 2, 2024, 100083, ISSN 2713-3745, https://doi.org/10.1016/j.yjoc.2024.100083

44. Marielle Segarra, "How to Make Your Nature Walks Even More Restorative, According to Science," NPR, April 22, 2025, https://www.npr.org/2023/08/22/1195337204/a-guide-to-forest-bathing.

45. Malcolm Gladwell, Blink: The Power of Thinking Without Thinking, 2018.

Part Three: Reclaiming the Future

46. Liz Mineo and Liz Mineo, "Why Employers Want Workers With High EQs," Harvard Gazette, August 29, 2025, https://news.harvard.edu/gazette/story/2025/08/what-is-emotional-intelligence-and-why-is-it-crucial-in-the-workplace/.